POETRY MATTERS

Edited by Claire Tupholme

Yorkshire & Lincolnshire

First published in Great Britain in 2011 by:

 Young**Writers**

Remus House
Coltsfoot Drive
Peterborough
PE2 9BF
Telephone: 01733 890066
Website: www.youngwriters.co.uk

Foreword

Since our inception in 1991, Young Writers has endeavoured to promote poetry and creative writing within schools by running annual nationwide competitions. These competitions are designed to develop and nurture the burgeoning creativity of the next generation, and give them valuable confidence in their own abilities.

This regional anthology is one of the series produced by our latest secondary school competition, *Poetry Matters*. Using poetry as their tool, the young writers were given the opportunity to tell the world what matters to them. The authors of our favourite three poems were also given the chance to appear on the front cover of their region's collection.

Whilst skilfully conveying their opinions through poetry, the writers showcased in this collection have simultaneously managed to give poetry a breath of fresh air, brought it to life and made it relevant to them. Using a variety of themes and styles, our featured poets leave a lasting impression of their inner thoughts and feelings, making this anthology a rare insight into the next generation.

Contents

Tollbar Edge Cleethorpes Academy, Cleethorpes

The Poems

What Matters To Me

What matters to me should matter to you
What crazy is, what crazy do
I'll tell you what matters to me
It's that we all think freely.

There are loads more things that matter to me
Like my school
It's not because I'm a sad old mule
I care about my life
Just because I want to strive for my grades
So I'll have a good job
And not stay at home on the sofa like a fat slob.

I want a house, money and a car
And not to be eating out of a jam jar
I want to live life and breathe air
And by the time I'm sixty I want all my hair
I don't want my life to pass me by
This is the end of my poem so bye-bye.

Ammaar Rashid (13)
Birkdale Senior School, Sheffield

Music

I can smell the sweat as I play the keyboard.
It's as black as King Kong and goes *ping, pong.*
My bass guitar is as yellow as the sun.
I can feel my thumb going *strum, strum, strum.*
My superb drum is as white as a fang
I can hear my drum going *bang, bang, bang.*
I can see my cymbal spinning around,
It's as gold as bling and it goes *ting, ting.*
I can taste fame from my electric guitar
It's as red as fire, the noise comes through an amplifier.

Jonathan Wilson (11)
Brigshaw High School, Allerton Bywater

Auntie

You were
Like a mother to me
You looked after me
You cared for me.

You were
Like a blanket to me
You kept me safe
And you protected me.

You were
Like a teddy bear to me
You kept me warm when I was cold
You cheered me up when I was down.

You were
Like an open locket to me
Capturing all the good memories
And seeing my good side.

You were
The sun in my sky
Always shining on me
Brightening my day
And making my life bright.

You were
The map that guided me
Changed my direction
And put me in the right place.

You were
My life, my heart, my soul.

Sinead Parker (15)
Brigshaw High School, Allerton Bywater

Let's Have A Party!

I know I don't seem to be such a smarty but the idea hit me,
let's have a party!
I'm going to invite everyone on the block,
the party will go on, it will never stop!
I run upstairs and bring down my saxophone,
we play along so I get my xylophone!
Everybody feeling good, everybody's dancing,
singing on the karaoke everybody's prancing!
But uh-oh! I hear a loud smash, it was the window,
now all the plates are going to *crash!*
All I can hear is *bash, bang, boom,*
and then outside I hear a car go *zoom, zoom!*
My parents are home, they've seen what I've done
I shout to everyone, 'Quick, run, run, run!'
They run to the garden and jump over the hedge,
some climb out the window and dangle off the ledge!
Now hurry think quick!
Time's going tick!
I move all the plates and stand on the table
I jump through the window and run to the stable!
Before I know it I am really warm,
I wake up and realise it is dawn!
I go downstairs the kitchen is clean,
I find out it was a really bad dream.
I think to myself, *if it's so very tidy,*
maybe I could have a very fun party!

Bethany Ellis (11)
Brigshaw High School, Allerton Bywater

Best Friends

You are like my sister
Sweet but stubborn
You are like my mornings
Easy but hard
You are like my moonlight
There when I'm scared at night
You are like my oxygen
There when I find it hard to breathe
You are like my laughter
Loud and clear
You are like my tear
Pure with no fear
You are like my life
When you cut me with the knife
But then you stand there with a plaster ready to heal
You are like my everything
I couldn't live without you
I love you.

Laura Smith-Whiteley (14)
Brigshaw High School, Allerton Bywater

Love . . .

Getting to know people is the colour of gold.
The laughter and jokes on your first date is a ha-ha.
The taste of chocolate is *crunch, crunch.*
The colour of happiness is rosy pink.
The warmth of your partner beside you is like summer again.
Valentine's Day has finally arrived for you and your loved one.
Marriage is like you were born all over again.
The smell of the after wedding party treats is a *sniff, sniff.*
The end of a long journey . . . *death.*

Megan Axall (11)
Brigshaw High School, Allerton Bywater

Sweet Shop Poem

The sweet shop as they say
Is where children spend their day
From box to box
And cup to cup
There's always somewhere you can look
The candy mice as white as snow
With sugary strips that always glow
The yellow sherbet tastes as strong as a lemon fruit
And teddy-shaped gummy bears that are so cute
The bubblegum tower was a rainbow
These sweets are most popular didn't you know!
The red stars cried when a girl scooped her
Into a pick 'n' mix bag
Every little sweet to eat has a price tag
The sweet shop down the road
It is the best and better than the rest
£2.60 please, thank you!

Kate Varley (11)
Brigshaw High School, Allerton Bywater

War

Hear the footsteps as the troops enter the battlefield
See the tanks as they move in to fight the enemy.
Hear the jets as they fly over you to bombard them.
Feel the fear as your body trembles with it.
Taste the feeling of being victorious.
Check your equipment to see if anything is missing.
Touch the trigger and check the ammunition. Ready to kill.
Enemies come out of the alleyway firing.
You raise your weapon going to fire.
Enemies on the rooftops raise your weapon higher, fire!
You get hit by a bullet and fall to the ground.
And you feel the blackness of death.

Billy Stevenson (11)
Brigshaw High School, Allerton Bywater

Praise Song For Elisha

You were
Sun to me
Bright, bold and always there.

You were
A flower to me
Beautiful and always going up.

You were
A rainbow to me
Opinionated and colourful.

You were
The sky's brightest star
The moon's shine
The beauty of the night.

You were always
There.

Sophie Impey [15]
Brigshaw High School, Allerton Bywater

My Perfect World

My perfect world, my perfect world would be as beautiful as a rose.
My perfect world, my perfect world would be as pretty as a rainbow.

Everyone would be friends and have a family,
No more violence, no screams of death,
And you would hear the cheers for the end of poverty!

The crashes and booms of war had stopped,
Animals were free to do what they want,
Drugs and binge-drinking had been dropped!

Everyone would get a full education and there would be equal rights for all!
But there's one great thing about today . . .

Everyone is different in their own way!

Antonia Brooks [11]
Brigshaw High School, Allerton Bywater

Praise Song For My Dad

You were
A rock to me,
Comforting,
Strong,
And always there.

You were
Like a fire to me,
Brave,
Heart-warming,
And never dull.

You were
Summer to me,
Friendly,
Happy,
And everlasting.

Ellie Scott (14)
Brigshaw High School, Allerton Bywater

My Bike!

You are
The light to me
Guiding me through the dark.

You are
The jaguar to me
Fast, furious and steady.

You are
Cold-blooded to me
The cold silent metal structure.

You are
The wheels of life to me
Grinding the dirt below me.

Danny Banks (14)
Brigshaw High School, Allerton Bywater

Praise Song For My Mum

You are
The sun's core to me,
Always there, shining rapidly.

You have
The shoulder I need to cry on
To wipe away the tears that fall.

You are
The blanket I use when cold,
Warm and thoughtful and cosy.

You are
The warmth of the sun,
The sparkle of the ocean,
The love of a pounding heart.

Forever and always.

Mollie Wilson (14)
Brigshaw High School, Allerton Bywater

Praise Song For My Mother

You are
Sun to me
Warm and cosy and blinding.

You are
An extra hand to me
Helping and generous and always there.

You are
A beating heart to me
Loving and caring and adored.

You are
Summer to me
Bright and happy and cheerful.

Jorja Dennison (14)
Brigshaw High School, Allerton Bywater

Mum

You are
A shooting star to me
You are one in a million years

You are
Blood to me
I wouldn't live without you.

You are
A castle wall to me
Strong and always help me when I need you.

You are
Sunshine to me
Bright and shining and always happy to me
Like a beautiful sunny day.

Ben Scargill (14)
Brigshaw High School, Allerton Bywater

The World Is . . .

The rock is
A towering body
Standing tall over the world.

The cloud is
A white bunny rabbit
Bouncing up and down in the sky.

The volcano is
A river of gushing lava
Swiftly and rapidly running down the side.

The world is
A place of destruction
Dying from global warming.

Heidi Thomas (11)
Brigshaw High School, Allerton Bywater

Dave's The Guy

You are the open book,
Knowledge for my eager mind.

You are the pit-bull man,
Yet a puppy lies inside.

You are the big fuzzy bear,
The one with the fishing rod.

You are the map to my success,
Showing me the hard ridden path.

You are an organ of mine,
A life long necessity.

You are Dave, the man I know!

Jordan Rowell (15)
Brigshaw High School, Allerton Bywater

Halloween

Halloween is the time for a scare,
People trick or treating everywhere,
'Trick or treat?' people say to others,
Even when they're with their mothers,
Witches cackle on their broomsticks,
Even though bands play the acoustic,
Pumpkins with their scary faces,
Everyone going to different places,
Bats flying in the air,
They don't want to share,
That is so unfair,
Halloween is ace,
I love Halloween!

Inka Clark (12)
Brigshaw High School, Allerton Bywater

A Brilliant Mum

You are so beautiful,
You are so kind,
You are small and lovely,
You are lovely and read my mind.

You are young and lovely,
You are young and small,
You finally have a boyfriend,
You are Cinderella at the ball.

You have blonde hair,
Bright as the sun,
Lovely and golden,
You are a brilliant mum.

Storm Wilkinson (12)
Brigshaw High School, Allerton Bywater

Praise Song For Uncle Neil

You are Red Bull to me,
You give me wings to ride my motocross bike.

You are a missile to me,
You have explosive energy on your 500cc KTM.

You are a teacher to me,
You teach me tricks and seat hops, also skills.

You are a leader to me,
I'll follow you over jumps to jump on the track.

You are water to me,
When we go for break you give me Red Bull I would not survive without.

Jack Hepworth (14)
Brigshaw High School, Allerton Bywater

Nature

The weeping willow wept,
While the salty sea slept.

The bush used gel,
Which I could smell.

Snow as white as paper,
One tree was called Draper.

Trees as green as grass,
But the dolphin was a lass.

Remember nature is great,
Under the Earth surface there are plates.

Amy Stevenson (11)
Brigshaw High School, Allerton Bywater

Red Is . . .

Delicate love filling many empty, angry hearts with joy and precious love!
Anger and hate from beneath our feet, down where the evil devils make
plans to rip and tear the hearts of the innocent!
Red-hot, mouth-burning chillies, they go in as a chilli and come out (of the
ears) as steam!
The wonderful memories of those who fight for us, packed in one single
flower, this magnificent flower goes by the name of a poppy!
Hot, blazing flames spreading everywhere in an instant!
A scarlet circular logo reading; Brigshaw High School!

Louisa Morley (11)
Brigshaw High School, Allerton Bywater

Red Is . . .

Red is the colour of lovers bonding, also the colour of a dying soldier.
Red is the colour of good old Santa.
Red is the colour of a precious ruby.
Red is the colour of your dad on holiday.
Red is the colour of a crunchy apple.
Red is the colour of a brand new baby.
Red is the colour of the sun above.
Red is the colour of Mum's lipstick.
Red is the colour of my T-shirt.

Alex Erskine (11)
Brigshaw High School, Allerton Bywater

Blue Is . . .

Blue is the sea,
Lapping over the sand.
Blue is the sky,
Filled with stars.
Blue is a man,
Down in the dumps.
Blue is all these things
And more.

Molly Hayward (11)
Brigshaw High School, Allerton Bywater

Days Of The Week Poem

Monday tastes of back to sandwiches
Tuesday looks like shuttlecocks everywhere from badminton club
Wednesday smells like sweat pouring down our faces from football club
Thursday sounds like our team coach
Friday feels like reincarnation as the weekend approaches.

Luke Wood (11)
Brigshaw High School, Allerton Bywater

The Rainbow

I've got a rainbow above my head, the first of its colours is bright red.
Then comes orange then yellow and green, the loveliest colours I've
ever seen.
Next comes blue, blue of the sea, indigo and violet are the others I see.
When the sun comes out through the falling rain
My rainbow makes a coloured arch above my counterpane.
Rainbow, rainbow come again soon, shine in my bedroom till the coming of
the moon.

Leah Passey (11)
Brigshaw High School, Allerton Bywater

Senses Of The Week

Monday tastes of delicious and delectable school dinners as we return to
school after the fun weekend.
Tuesday smells of sweat after our energetic PE lesson and badminton club.
Wednesday sounds like the teacher telling us what to do during the
school day.
Thursday looks like the PlayStation and the FIFA II game which I usually
play on after a school day.
Friday feels like rugby balls as we do a rough session of rugby during PE.

Ryan Gledhill (11)
Brigshaw High School, Allerton Bywater

Red Is . . .

R ed is the colour of a vampire feast
E very animal and human awakens to a red beast
D emolished by fire, anger or ink

I gnited by royalty and power
S pecial dreams stir from red pulling you in for an adventure but never in
   order to cower.

Eleanor Richardson (11)
Brigshaw High School, Allerton Bywater

Red Is . . .

R ed is . . . an angry red dinosaur coming to get me with,
E ggs painted red to look like blood cells and then the red dinosaur was
going to hit me with them.
D inosaurs take the eggs, painted as red blood cells, off the shelf and start
to throw them at me, can I cope in the land of red . . .

No, who could live in the land of red, oh let me think, an angry red
dinosaur can. Ha-ha!

Emma Wadsworth (11)
Brigshaw High School, Allerton Bywater

Red Is . . .

Red is a rose drenched in love.
Red is an angry Liverpool fan shouting at Santa who is hiding in a postbox
drinking Coca-Cola.
Red is a vampire's delight.
Red is Satan living in the flame ridden depths of Hell.
Red is a fiery Ferrari.
Red is a wonderful colour.

Jordan Smart (11)
Brigshaw High School, Allerton Bywater

Saturday Senses

On a typical Saturday afternoon . . .
I can see 35,000 Leeds fans marching on together,
I can hear them singing and chanting whatever the weather,
The aroma of pies, hotdogs and beer makes me lick my lips,
At half-time I look forward to eating delicious, over-priced chips,
I sit so close to the players I can almost touch,
I want to play for Leeds very much.

Oliver Scales (11)
Brigshaw High School, Allerton Bywater

Red Is . . .

Red is loving, angry and kind,
Red is a problem on your mind.
Satan, blood, Ferrari and all,
Red is a colour we can't ignore.
Red is my juice in a water bottle,
Red is a crab in the mouth of an otter.

Georgia Kelly (11)
Brigshaw High School, Allerton Bywater

Red Is . . .

Red is . . . a rose dripping with blood.
Red is . . . the Devil living in the fiery pits of Hell.
Red is . . . an angry man wearing a Man Utd shirt.
Red is . . . a Ferrari running over a postbox.
Red is . . . Santa filling Christmas stockings with Coke.
Red is . . . the colour of the Brigshaw logo.

Noah Hastings (11)
Brigshaw High School, Allerton Bywater

The Wonderful Sea

The sea is a lion's roar.
The sea is a giant hotel.
The sea is a huge water bed.
The sea is a shark's restaurant.
The sea is a gigantic blue quilt.
The sea is many, many things.

Jojo Connelly (11)
Brigshaw High School, Allerton Bywater

Red Is . . .

Red is a chunky KitKat ready to be eaten
Red is Liverpool fans chanting Man Utd are rubbish
Red is a Royal Mail postbox
Red is Satan drinking Coke in a chimney
Red is blood dripping from Satan's mouth
Red is a fiery Ferrari speeding down London's street.

Connor Briggs (12)
Brigshaw High School, Allerton Bywater

War

When the soldiers get on the aeroplane
They're thinking of their family as they did every day.
With guns in their hands not thinking of death
But when they get off, *bang, bang*, it's bullets over their heads.
With their loved ones at home feeling sad and wanting them back,
The smell of victory is close by but is it close enough?

Leah Wood (11)
Brigshaw High School, Allerton Bywater

Weekday Senses

Monday tastes of mouth-watering mints
Tuesday smells of sweat from PE
Wednesday sounds like my cousin screaming
Thursday looks like geography's coming
Friday feels like the weekend at last.

Georgia Brook (11)
Brigshaw High School, Allerton Bywater

To My Secret Love

You are the reason why I wake up in the morning
And why I try to look good every day
No matter what I do I think of you
I just wish it were the same, from your point of view
Because to you I'm just a friend.

Ben Hepworth (14)
Brigshaw High School, Allerton Bywater

Weather

The sun is a boiling heart
The moon is a rustic candle
The snow is God's frozen tears
The rain is the Earth's shower
The cloud is the world's blanket.

Frances Heap (11)
Brigshaw High School, Allerton Bywater

Untitled

My school car is shouting to go
I know it is slow
Honk, honk goes the horn
I saw a newborn.

Daniel Kyle Sadd (11)
Brigshaw High School, Allerton Bywater

My Mum Is What Matters To Me

When she smiles
It makes me smile
When she cries
It makes me wonder why.

When she cooks
She doesn't use cookery books
She shops lots
And I love her lots and lots.

When I see her she makes me happy
But sometimes she can be snappy
I love it when she bakes
She makes the best cakes
I love her so much
She has the most loving touch.

Last thing at night
She says sleep tight
When I drink my tea
She says goodbye to me
She goes to work
With a sudden jerk.

When she comes home
I am not alone
I make her laugh
As she walks up the garden path
We walk to the shop
But don't buy a lot
My mum is what matters to me.

Kimberley Whiteley (14)
Carleton Community High School, Pontefract

What Matters To Me

What matters to me
Is my ability to see
The sense to touch
And hear as much
I like to feel the cold air
Rushing through my hair.

I enjoy going on long walks
Taking my camera
Zooming the world into a square
That can be shared
At a moment's glare.

I like to see the sun rising
From the east
Awakening from its dream
And disappearing to the west
While the birds are performing.

But of course my family matters
The way they are always there
Even if they're not needed
You know they care.

The little things that could matter
The clothes that you wear
Your individuality
The way you treat others
And how you are there.

Fable Bramley-Blackburn (13)
Carleton Community High School, Pontefract

The Mind

Some are evil
Some are kind
But all great minds must think alike
For at this time
It should be mine
Then the world would surely see
How I could create a philosophy.

Maybe if the mind could think
How the danger can reform
And how it will forever link
Because of this shameful tyranny.

After all this time and we still don't know
How the mind can use its ways
To hold its nerve just to show
What it's seen throughout its days.

How the mind can remember
How it created the psychotic ember
Then it can make it stop
To make a peaceful world to drop.

Alex Murray (13)
Carleton Community High School, Pontefract

My Nan!

A picture of my nan is what matters to me,
The way she smiles as she's holding me.

How proud she was before
She was taken away!

She looked after me and held me tight,
It was so special the way she gently kissed me goodnight.

She was lovely and warm,
Pretty and kind!
I'll never forget her,
She's always on my mind.

The way she talked and the way she walked
Just made me smile.

But she was cold,
She was timid,
She was scared
And she was old.
Therefore I knew it was the end
And time for you to descend.

Toni Lloyd (13)
Carleton Community High School, Pontefract

What Matters To Me?

The stars in the sky have to be bright,
Asleep in the day and shine in the night.
The dog has to wake you at 4am
Then fall back to sleep again.

The winter's breeze has to be cold,
Grandma's TV has to be old.
Friday has to be the longest day,
The snow on Christmas has to lay.

Heavy footsteps has to be Dad,
The end of a movie has to be sad,
Must have a friend who's completely crazy
Must have a pet that's really lazy.

On a barbecue it always rains,
Your car gets stuck down country lanes,
With the good there's always the bad,
With the happy there is always the sad.

When the sun is gone and the rain is pouring,
At least we know it's never boring.

Kayleigh Maughan (13)
Carleton Community High School, Pontefract

Why?

Why is the Earth round?
Why were we made?
Why do we talk the way we do?
Why do people ask questions?

Why do we walk?
Why do we all look different?
Why do we have an imagination?
Why do we eat other animals?

Why do floods and earthquakes happen?
Why is the world made of whys?
Why do we forget things?
And the biggest why of all is . . .
Why?

Megan Haycock [13]
Carleton Community High School, Pontefract

My Best Friend

My best friend, well what can I say?
Apart from the way you tell me everything
And a million times more
To be honest, if I didn't have you,
I think I'd be a wreck,
But you're the best friend that laughs when I fall,
And cries when I'm sad . . .
You are the first person I turn to with all my problems,
I don't know whether to laugh or cry,
As you're the only person I can call family.
Yeah, sure, we've had our ups and downs
But now, closer than *ever!*
I love you, promise me nothing will ever change.

Hannah Leadbeater [13]
Carleton Community High School, Pontefract

The Night

There's something special about the night.
It's different.
Some people might fear it
But I feel there is nothing to be feared
Perhaps they are too scared of discovering it
For me, the night is peaceful yet exciting
And magical in so many ways.
The sky is beautiful on a night -
It really speaks to me - volumes in fact!
When I can see the stars on a crystal-clear night,
It's so enchanting.
It's nothing a painting or photo could capture
You need to be there!
I like cloudy nights too,
The clouds add an air of mystery
To the sky.
Starry nights are the best though - it's magical to watch them.
I can get stuck in a world just looking at the stars;
It opens a new world for me.
At night I feel nothing is impossible
But I also feel worried by unnecessary bad thoughts
Playing on my mind.
I think now I understand why people are scared of the dark
Or the night,
Maybe they yearn to discover it but are too scared.
They probably want comfort in their bed.
Normality.
Me however, I'd rather discover the magic world
But instead watch the sky.
Maybe one night I will discover it, maybe one night.

Katie Webster (13)
Corpus Christi Catholic College, Leeds

Best Friends

Knowing someone's there,
To offer you their care,
To help and guide you through,
They make you feel brand new.

Best friends,
Building dens,
Having fun,
Feeling young.

She helps you along the way,
When you're struggling through the day,
To listen when you're sad,
Or when you're moaning 'bout your dad.

Best friends,
Keeping up with trends,
Having a laugh,
Calling Dad naff!

They text you when you're sick,
And stop people taking the mick.
They help you with your maths,
Drawing pictures of giraffes.

Best friends,
Fun never ends,
Staying out,
Messing about.

Then you remember when,
You both looked after Ben,
You were acting like a fool,
She just acted cool.

Best friends,
Well it depends,
Of course,
Don't be a horse!

We used to like the same toys
But now we like the same boys,
Now we know,

When we're low,
That we've got each other
And our mothers.

I'm Amy,
And she's Jamie,
That's why we're
Best friends
Till the end!

Amy Lyons (13)
Corpus Christi Catholic College, Leeds

Love

Love is a rare thing,
It is lovely in the spring!

It makes you feel all warm inside,
And it happens when in comes the tide.

As we walk along the bitty sand,
We walk and walk hand in hand.

I look above and see doves flying high,
Could it be a symbol that sparks will fly?

He is very dearest to me is my man,
But sometimes I feel like hitting him with a frying pan!

When I see him I give him a special look,
The kind you give when you've just finished a book.

There are many different types of love,
But this one is like wearing a glove.

It is warm and cuddly,
Which is just lovely!

So I hope one day you find it,
And don't regret it one bit!

Amy Morgan (13)
Corpus Christi Catholic College, Leeds

I, The Lonely One

It was today, was the day,
When I had apparently died,
And I was as happy as could be,
You know, I could've cried!
It was today, was the day, that
When I had died
Well apparently I had died
As I lied - or tried.
Now, when it was today, the day I died.
I was sat in the corner,
Where no one's eyes pried.
Cos people thought I was different,
You know in the head,
But I hadn't done nothing wrong
What've I said?
I was playing with my Lego
Like I did every day,
And then someone came over and killed me
I mean, what did I say?
But I don't know if I'm missing something,
You know cos I'm mad.
Well, I wouldn't call me mental - well maybe a tad!
But the thing is people don't know me
They run away from me kind of like I'm a flea!
'Don't worry, my lad,' my father said
'I'll be with you until the day you're dead.'
Well now I'm dead I'm really sad
Cos basically, I'll never see my dad
But back to the school, the place I had died
I never thought I'd say that
I wish it could be washed away by the tide.
But I'm not normal, you see.
The people in my class, they laugh at me.
They call me names that I don't know,
So I just smile and on I go
How am I to understand?
The things that go on and get out of hand.
Almost like what killed me

I don't even know what happened you see?
I wish I could have told you more
But something in my heart just tore
I think it was the place where the bullet hit
In the place in the corner where I did sit
Or it could be the pain in me
The bullying is the pain, you see.

Gage Oxley (13)
Corpus Christi Catholic College, Leeds

The Child In Him

I love the child in him
So innocent and sweet
The mischief in his eyes
The blush upon his cheek
The tender way he spoke
That showed me that he cared
The touch of his warm hand
That gently touched my hair
The smiles that we shared
That filled my heart with glee
For when I was with him
I found the child in me.

If all I know should fall apart
There is one thing deep at heart
That in this world one thing was true
I will always be in love with you.

I never knew about happiness
I didn't think dreams came true
I couldn't believe in love
Until I finally met you.

Jamie Allanson (13)
Corpus Christi Catholic College, Leeds

The Best Way To Be, Is To Be

Like a thief in the night, death steals away,
With a loved one, maybe old and grey,
Or a young girl crying on her bed,
Thoughts racing around her mind,
Thinking, *why can't the other girls be more kind?*
Then she lifts the gun up to her head,
Pulls the trigger, *bang . . .* now she's dead
And with death came eternal happiness,
And I wonder if she'll make a beautiful corpse.

But if she had heard the other girls' cries,
When they had learned of her demise,
Would she have changed her decision?
Would she have changed the gun's precision?
But it's too late to change it now,
Her decision changed the life,
Of everyone she ever met,
And if she had, I would bet,
She wouldn't have raised the knife,
And caused the people such despair,
For her friends it was too much to bear.

Like a thief in the night, death steals away,
With a loved one, maybe old and grey,
Or the young girl crying on her bed,
Wishing, wishing she was dead,
But if she looks ahead she'll see,
The best way to be, is to be.

Charlotte Butler (13)
Corpus Christi Catholic College, Leeds

Potterton Park

They ask, why do I go
In snow, sun or rain
To repeat the ritual
Again and again
Where the duty of care
Is always the same
I go to forget all my
Trouble and pain.

Struggle with words
And descriptions in books
No verse can describe
The flight of the rooks
Silhouettes in the sky
Avoiding the ducks
And the grounded humans
And envious looks.

There in my paradise
Away from the glare
At Potterton Park
With its foxes and hares
And my own darling Honey
My own chestnut mare
Harmony and peace
I've found hiding there.

Gabi Fallon (13)
Corpus Christi Catholic College, Leeds

The Ear

I have an ear
It helps me hear
It's simple but needed and works.

Conor Bradley (14)
Corpus Christi Catholic College, Leeds

Snooker!

Snooker, snooker it's such a great game,
Compare the players, they're just not the same,
With Alex Higgins and Jimmy White,
If you saw them play, 'twas a brilliant sight.

When you're playing snooker,
You hit the ball to go in the pocket.
That's why they call Ronnie the Rocket.
He bends and swerves the balls around,
Playing left-handed or right, he stands his ground.

World Champion is the aim of their game,
Collecting the money and enjoying the fame.
A kiss and a miss, a snooker and a pot,
Mind ticking over what a brilliant shot.

From the Crucible in Sheffield their confidence grows,
So come on lads, give us a good show.
From Stephen Hendry or Steve Davis,
And from John Parrott or John Higgins,
Just to name a few,
Depending on the game and who they drew.

Peter Clarke (13)
Corpus Christi Catholic College, Leeds

Chiron

Oh so alone, the centaur roams
Astray from all the other centaur's homes
He gallops and strides, like the rest of the gang
But unlike the others, he was not yin but yang.

He was clever and noble and held such knowledge
He was skilled with medicine and fluent in language
Unlike the others, he was gentle and kind
Never violent, his personality shone.

Every other centaur was eager to fight
Extremely violent and stupid, quite!
Great in battle
But arrogant at heart,
Impressively strong but not very smart.

So the centaur that stood out from the rest
His name was Chiron, and he often stressed
That he could never fit in with any of the others
But he never realised how good it was
To be different from his brothers.

Catherine Joyce (13)
Corpus Christi Catholic College, Leeds

Death

Death
Voices calling my name,
I feel cold,
My existence is becoming old.

My heart beating slower and slower,
My eyes fading into blind.
I begin to feel tired,
My body is no longer wired.

A blood puddle spreading,
All of this I was dreading,
Where am I going?
This is my unknowing.

Without any way to keep myself in control,
My future story is untold,
No longer may I dwell,
Death has taken me to the gates of Hell.

I am dead.

Alex Querishi (13)
Corpus Christi Catholic College, Leeds

Gangster's Gamble

To the table I go,
The cards are given,
My name is Joe,
Cheaters are ridden.

Just like in Casino,
De Niro's great
I'm wanted in Reno,
It's my fate.

I'm the best at what I do,
The dealer says it is he,
My opponents in view,
So deal the cards and we shall see what will be.

It's near the end of the game,
I have won,
I keep my fame,
With the threat of my gun!

Callum Gunn (13)
Corpus Christi Catholic College, Leeds

Rainbows

Rainbows are beautiful, sparkly and bright.
But they only come when the conditions are right.
When it rains and pours but the sun shines too.
This is when rainbows are usually due.

There are lots of different stories about pots of gold.
But you shouldn't always listen to what you've been told.
This is one of the stories that they often may teach.
But the end of the rainbow is never in reach.

The colours you see are vivid and bright.
To remember them all is hard to get right.
Richard of York gave battle in vain.
Learn this, you'll never forget them again.

All different colours maybe red and green.
But it doesn't stay forever so when you've seen.
A bright shiny rainbow in the sky.
Make a wish and then say goodbye.

Megan Scanlon (13)
Corpus Christi Catholic College, Leeds

Space

S olar systems, stars and the vast beyond.
P lanets soaring of which I am fond.
A steroids orbiting all through the night.
C ircling planets and stars - such a sight.
E xcept in the morning, when night goes without a warning.

Isabelle O'Dowd (13)
Corpus Christi Catholic College, Leeds

The Beach

The sun rises lighting up the sky.
Fluffy white clouds hover in the air above.
As the sea rustles, the waves crash against the chalky cliffs.
Footprints appear in the squelchy sand.
A city of sandcastles stand on the smooth flaky ground.
Deckchairs stand lonely by the shore.
Families sit down for an afternoon picnic.
Hundreds of beach balls fly through the sky
Children swim in the glistening sea.
Black shadows slither under the deep blue sea.

Every beach has a heart full of love,
A smile full of joy
And is full of happiness.

Sarah McBeth (13)
Corpus Christi Catholic College, Leeds

The Tapping

When studying on a cold frosty night
There came a tapping at the door
So gentle was the tapping that the moment passed by
Until I heard another tapping louder than before
Then quietened until it could not be heard above the wind
I tried to forget about the tapping on the door
But I only reminded myself more
When all of a sudden came a slam at the door
Then a knock
Then a tap
Then a whisper
Then nothing
Then I opened the door.

Luke Jackson (13)
Corpus Christi Catholic College, Leeds

Apples

Apples are tasty,
I think they are nice.
I like to consume them,
Each day once or twice.

They grow on big trees,
There are many different kinds.
They can be green or red,
And they improve people's minds.

So when you're having chocolate,
When you're about to take a bite,
Just think for one second,
Ooh an apple! I just might.

Hung Quoc Diep (14)
Corpus Christi Catholic College, Leeds

From Summer To Summer

Grass swirled beneath my feet
Trees rattled to the distant beat
Birds chirped as the sun rose
Insects swerved around my toes.

The flowers were strange with a bright glow
Better than the ground being covered in snow.

Some live
Some die
Some come to stay
Some pass by
People are like plants,
We need water to grow,
We need to change to let go.

Megan Clark (13)
Danum School, Doncaster

My Trip To Wembley

We got on the bus
We all made a fuss
We were on our way to Wembley
Our sandwiches made,
Kits proudly displayed
For the match between Man Utd and Chelsea.
Many chances were made
As the game was played.
Then Valencia scored a screamer
The Chelsea fans went quiet
As we caused a riot
Cheering and throwing streamers
Two more goals came
During the game
From Berbatov and Scholes
Man Utd were winning
United fans were singing
And Chelsea only scored one goal
We had such a good day
And went on our way
On the coach for the long journey home.

Curtis Hamshaw (12)
Danum School, Doncaster

It Doesn't Matter

It doesn't matter how things fly, crawl or float in the sky.
I am always there to sing my lullaby
It doesn't matter when clouds float in the dreamy sky
Or when birds sing and fly by
It doesn't matter when lizards crawl upon the dusty ground
Or when I shout, 'Oh look, some gold I've found.'
It doesn't matter how things fly, crawl or float in the sky.
I am always there to sing my lullaby.

Jade Elizabeth Duffield (12)
Danum School, Doncaster

Great Grandad

Tears have fallen for you,
Some happy, some sad,
A man that grew up to love,
A man that I called my great grandad.
How I wish you were still here
To see me grow old,
Although it won't be like yours.
I'll have a story told.
The day you went,
Was a day of grieving,
Didn't want to think of life without you,
Knowing that you were leaving.
How I miss you so much,
I didn't think I would cope
I suppose I was wrong,
There is God to give us hope.
Though I cannot see you,
I know you're still here,
In my memories you will always live,
In my heart you're always near.

Simran Singh (14)
Danum School, Doncaster

The Future

The future is bleak
But our love is not weak
The future will change
But my love for you will not,
Not now nor ever.
Whatever comes of the future
Whatever happens to me and you
We will fight on, fight through,
Forever and always together.

Harry Pearson (15)
Danum School, Doncaster

40

Maybe . . .

I watched you as you walked
As you just passed by,
Your face sparkled,
As the sun shone.

I saw you as you smiled,
Watched as you looked up to the sky,
All your dreams in front of you,
And just have to try.

The day fell to night,
As you glanced up at the stars
You wished you were there
You hoped to be that far.

That was what you wanted,
You wanted to be free,
And maybe I was wrong,
Maybe that was me.

Gemma Haigh (14)
Danum School, Doncaster

School Days

Waking up at seven o'clock,
Go back to sleep for a few tick-tocks.
Wake up again, get in the shower,
Feel the splashing, the water, the power,
Get out, get dressed, takes about half an hour.
Now I'm ready for school and I'm not gonna cower.
Grab my keys, lock the door,
Waiting to unlock it again about half-past four,
Run upstairs, get changed into some jeans
And a brand new T-shirt, that looks really mean
After that I go out to see some people walk past the church with the big tall
steeple.

Tom Wilson (14)
Danum School, Doncaster

Sweet And Sour

You are like an angel,
So giving and so true,
No wonder everyone wants to spend,
Each second of each day with you.

You are like a diamond,
You sparkle like the sun,
You can light up the day with a single word,
And darken it by saying not one.

You are like a demon,
A raging fire sent from Hell,
Come to burn down my hopes and dreams,
And steal my self-confidence, as well.

Never again will I let it happen;
With myself I've made a pact.
To never again let myself be fooled,
By your sweet and sour act.

Hollie Marshall (15)
Danum School, Doncaster

Untitled

Inside she still loves him after all this time
And even though her heart bears the scars
That show no sign of healing
It's alright because she's loving him still after all this time.
She tries for the sake of it
Hopes for the sake of it
And still loves him for the sake of it,
She sees people walking by,
Families, couples and lovers,
And that's what she wants after all this time
She doesn't care how long it takes
She will still be loving him for all time.

Nathan Platts (14)
Danum School, Doncaster

13

When we were younger they asked us,
What we wanted to do.
Singer, dancer or actor?
An astronaut on the moon?

But now that I'm 13,
Life has taken its toll
So how's this for an answer?
Who the hell knows.

13 is not superstitious,
At least it's not for me,
Because now that I'm 13 years old,
I'm the best I'll ever be.

Charlotte Utting (13)
Danum School, Doncaster

I Miss You

I never go a day without thinking about you
I miss the way you smiled at me
Whenever I was down
I miss the way you smelt like TCP
Even though I didn't like it
I miss the way your eyes sparkled and lit up my day
I wish that we were closer but I'm just glad to say
I had you in my life and I wouldn't have had it any other way
Whenever I am sad and don't know what to do
I think of you and my worries disappear
I miss you and I will never forget you.

Emma Shaw (14)
Danum School, Doncaster

Ocean At Night

The foaming shingle sways back and forth,
Soaking up the sand with its absorbing claws,
Flyspeck grains of cream powder crumble,
Under tiny speeds of torrential sea.

A fluorescence of night covers the surface,
Forming cocoons of eternal shelter.
Now the aglow of scintilla beams will freeze,
Once the modern lighthouse lies down to rest.

Hannah Shaw (16)
Danum School, Doncaster

History Poem

Historians study things of the past
It's just like a play with a very large cast
Learning things of how the world used to be
And how the changes affect you and me
History will never grow old
There will always be a story to be told
Whether it's great leaders, wars, kings or queens
History is for all whether young, old or kids in their teens.

Bethany Louise Almond (12)
Danum School, Doncaster

Chokin Gall

Love is indeed a choking gall filled with unsatisfied passion.
Does love destroy its path while leaving the lover dumbfounded?
He waits on her to arrive but her arrival is black and portentous.
I never saw true beauty which hates to this day.
Love, cast your burden off me
But I indeed want to be in your hold
Out of your hold is my life out of this earth
The crows slander around my castle
But your dove takes advantage of me refusing them
The sun, fair sun rises to shine beauty on you.
But, your beauty too strong for the sun to outshine.
Brighter than gold or glitter
The roses grow in my heart, rose-a-line, they grow as your hatred for me
multiplies
If it is a crime to love, crown me the highest confused criminal
Destiny, bring us now together.
Peaceful hate fills your heart about me
But as the dove waits on its baby, as the penguins work in unison
As the sunflowers turn to the sun
As the rain calms the desert,
As the moon embraces the night
So my love to you will be
Sweeter than honey shall it be
The trees will wave at our joy and the clouds will gather to rain laughter on
us
And my footprints won't ever leave your heart.
For the greatest love comes from devotion
When it's time to go sleep in love.

Oyindasola Famodoun
Fir Vale School, Sheffield

Let Me Free Of My Leash

Let me free of my leash,
Let me go,
I want to live my life with freedom,
Not like a comedy show.

You've locked me up in chains,
And you've put me behind bars,
You're giving me the pains that I don't deserve,
You're chilling out in your fancy cars.

Let me free of my leash,
Let me go,
I want to live my life with freedom,
Not like a comedy show.

I'm not the one that should be living this life,
In fact it should be you,
You don't care about others and their feelings,
I can't wait till my wishes come true.

Let me free of my leash,
Let me go,
I want to live my life with freedom,
Not like a comedy show.

The day I walk out of here,
Owning my human rights
You will know that you did wrong
And what I did was right.

Let me free of my leash,
Let me go,
I want to live my life with freedom,
Not like a comedy show.

So wait till I get out of here with my dignity and pride,
Slavery is the answer to nothing,
You shouldn't change our human rights.

Let me free of my leash,
Let me go,
I want to live my life with freedom,
Not like a comedy show.

It doesn't matter what colour you are,
Or where you are from,
Remember when you're worried,
You've got a dom.

Let me free of my leash,
Let me go,
I want to live my life with freedom,
Not like a comedy show.

Don't run away from life saying
'It's over, we've lost,'
Instead turn the other cheek,
Say:
'Give me what you've got!'

Let me free of my leash,
Let me go,
I want to live my life with freedom,
Not like a comedy show.

You can win!

Sana Khan (12)
Fir Vale School, Sheffield

Birds

The birds fly free in the sky
Swooping, soaring, swishing
Their wings spread out like
Angels, their slim bodies silhouetted
Against the electric blue sky.

The birds fly free in the sky
Swooping, soaring, swishing
Until in the winter
They go to far-off places.
Then in summer they come back to us.

Jess Hanson (12)
Fir Vale School, Sheffield

Autumn

Autumn blue
Autumn grey
Autumn sing
Autumn stay

Autumn leaves
Autumn rain
Autumn fun
With no pain

Autumn trees
Autumn breeze
Autumn sneeze
Autumn bees

Autumn sky
Autumn dark
Autumn birds
Autumn spark

Autumn days
Autumn plays
Autumn season
Forever stays.

Taisha Maneus (13)
Fir Vale School, Sheffield

Mother

You wake me up in the morning with a beautiful smile on your face,
Then you laugh at me because I look a disgrace.
You wash my face and brush my teeth,
I'm so lucky to have you I'm in sudden grief!
You are my gorgeous mother,
My sweet gentle lover,
The sweetness in my heart,
Which makes us part,
The smile on my chin,
The one who tells God to forgive me because of my sin.
The lightness of the sun,
The tastiness of my favourite bun.
You are my smile, laughter and fun,
All put together I'm in stun,
I will never forget you,
Even when I die,
It will always be true,
No it's not a lie,
It's just that:
I love you!

Adeela Ahmed (12)
Fir Vale School, Sheffield

The Lost Angel

Deep down in the dark woods,
Is an angel sitting in a tree.
Flying, swooping from all danger,
Caused by folk like you and me.

Constantly being followed,
And when she is hurt she hoots in sorrow.
Cries for her loved ones,
Like there is no tomorrow.

Her graceful elegance,
Can be the end of many things.
A death sentence for rodents,
Carried on silent wings.

But when she hears that lethal bang,
Guns fire, bullets rain.
In robes that gleam with winter sheen,
The snow-white owl to Heaven again.

Riona Shergold (11)
Fir Vale School, Sheffield

Love At First Sight

The first time I saw you I fell in love with you,
How I saw you was just like magic as if it was predicted,
A blink of an eye and there you were, the most beautiful rose,
I tried to learn it; I tried to say it, is it that hard to say I love you,

Once I helped you, you thought it was gratitude,
When I saved you, you thought it was friendship,
Then I kissed you, finally it was love,
But the blossoming of a rose and the withering of another,

I had ruined your future relationship the one you wished for,
I did not hear, I did not know, I did not know you didn't like me,
There was another boy in your mind,
Much more superior and strong,

But may I say no one will love you more than me,
Now I cannot approach you, I cannot look at you,
I can never repent to what I have done,
I bid you farewell, my first and only love.

Faisal Awadh (12)
Fir Vale School, Sheffield

My Family!

Before I sleep, a few days a week
I lie in my bed then feel a breeze
Jump out of bed and on my knees
Put my hands together
I trust the dear God make burglars beware.
I could lose all I gained, could even lose me life
Have you done that before is that what you've framed
What's the point, do you get paid?
Innocent lives, easily lost, hard to get
The beginning and end is so much pain
I love them dear God, please make them obey
Obey the law and make them say
Forgive me dear God for what I've done today,
I promise I'll not do it again.

Thank you God for listening.
Amen.

Keeley Rodda (11)
Fir Vale School, Sheffield

Them

I saw them staring at me with their sharp dagger eyes,
Looking at me like I am not human, a creature from out of space,
Laughing at me all day long,
Saying that the clothes I wear are weird and just wrong,
Saying that I cannot speak for now I wish I couldn't
Hearing the things they say about me,
With me as their main target,
For I feel sorry for those who have been their prey,
As I walk home I see the smirks on their faces,
Then I start to increase my pace,
Giving me dirty looks as they see me in the room,
With me hoping that it will end soon,
And now I have ended it for good,
Me hanging there still, pale, deathly as ever before.

Ayishah Khan (12)
Fir Vale School, Sheffield

The Start Of Spring

A beautiful woman
She lies in her bed, slowly waking
Stirring slightly, beginning to come alive
She drifts in and out of sleep
Unpredictable
She knows she must wake up soon.

Her eyes open
Look left, then right
And smiles out to everything, everyone
And she thinks to herself,
Hello world, it's my turn now
She opens her mouth
And takes the first breath of pure spring air.

Carys Thomas
Fir Vale School, Sheffield

Depression

A mere step, thought, smile, mask
Laughter, swagger, beauty, contribution
Too much to ask
Too difficult to apply
Too little to want

One toned, one view, one dreadful feeling
Hideous, numb and warmless
Cataclysmically paralysed, I am weaning
Weaning myself away from the conscious
Bringing my mind closer to its inner darkness

Stop, concentrate, live, learn, respond.
Leave it behind.

Nicholl Hardwick (18)
Grimsby Institute of Further & Higher Education, Grimsby

Let Me Know

I once had a hope, a dream,
Where now I have nothing.

On this street I walk past the remnants of shattered hearts,
Built on the foundations of broken dreams.
In this life, Loneliness and Disappointment are only the next adventure.

Then through the colossal holes we travel,
To go to the place where we end our days.
A lonely walk to turn into my friendly socialisation
But if there is more to this story please let me know.

Alex Witham (16)
Grimsby Institute of Further & Higher Education, Grimsby

What Matters To Me

What matters to me;
it may not matter to you,
just as long as you see my point of view,

your hopes and dreams
may not be what they seem,
but if you don't try,
you'll never know why,

fashion is opinion,
style is real,
music is choice,
and the way you feel,

family is love,
helping me rise above,
where my dreams lie,
in the sky,

if I stay with my friends,
I'll be here at the end,
if I don't maybe I won't,
we'll have to see,
I'm just being me,
that's all I can do,
just you be you.

Amber Wray (13)
Handsworth Grange School, Sheffield

I Believe In . . .

I believe in music, it helps you in a way in life you just can't see,
it tells a story and gives different emotions
that you can feel yourself,
it always has a beginning and an end.

I believe in my family and friends,
they can be there to support me every step of the way,
if I'm doing something or just through life itself.
As long as they can have a laugh, everything's fine.

I believe in your attitude, it can stop you in a way of life,
you just don't know,
it feels like you don't care about what other people think,
but deep down you do.

I believe in the health in people,
good health and bad health.
Your friends should always be there,
as long as you know they're alright, you're alright.

I believe in peace where it's calm and quiet,
where everyone is equal but not the same.

This is my poem and my advice through life to come.
Thanks for listening.

Elliott Sherwin (13)
Handsworth Grange School, Sheffield

What Matters To Me

I like apples, they're as juicy as the dew fall
I adore music it's like chocolate to my ears.

Paper City. People lonely.
Just trash getting swept up with the dirt.

Not heard, not seen.
The beat of people stamping their feet makes them fall.
The words 'hate', 'destroyed' come back on their paper body.
People spitting on them like they're not even there.
Just ignored.

What matters to me is making people happy
and not just like paper with words of hate written on them.

Charlotte Brown (14)
Handsworth Grange School, Sheffield

What Matters To Me

I believe in my friends' happiness and the sound of someone smiling.
I love it when someone gives me a hug,
it fills my heart with laughter.
It angers me when someone is hurt or sad.
I believe in happily ever after and to die with the one you love.
I believe you should stick to your wedding vows
and hate a cheating man.
I admire Nigella Lawson she is my idol, I love cooking so much,
the smell of something cooking makes my nose go crazy
and when I taste it my taste buds can't take it.
I love the world and everyone in it, we are all equal.

Holly Hallewell (13)
Handsworth Grange School, Sheffield

I Believe

I believe that free running is the world.
I feel like a bird flying free
I feel like I am alone running wild
I love boots because they give you the running edge
I hate when you get the biggest walls
They are like giants
I admire David Belle because he's the best thing ever
When I free run
I feel I can achieve the world
I feel I am invincible.

Travis Moulds (13)
Handsworth Grange School, Sheffield

I Believe

I believe in laughter
I believe in friends
I believe in people that listen to you
I trust in friends that trust in you.
My mind has gone boom
It can't be disguised
I'm trying to convince myself that I can concentrate
But my mind goes elsewhere
But for now it will have to do.

Dylan Driver (13)
Handsworth Grange School, Sheffield

Friendship

Friends are great,
don't have hate
for they are your friends,
they're part of your life.

They're always there for you,
whenever you need them,
but it's not just friends,
it's family too,
they're always there,
you can't get away.

They're there when you need them,
they're there when you don't
but either way,
they won't stay away.

They will get annoying,
and get stressed out,
but no matter what,
they won't leave you out.

Friends are great,
family too,
don't have hate,
for they're part of you.

Lauren Gledhill (13)
Immanuel CE Community College, Idle

My Family

I love my family because they love me.
My mum's cooking is brilliant!
My dogs are cute.
My brother beats me up for a laugh
And they all love me lots!

Tara Smith (11)
Immanuel CE Community College, Idle

What Matters To Me

What matters to me
is as sweet as can be.
I love my friends
I hope that never ends.
I adore my music
I try not to abuse it.
I love my cat
even though it's lazy and fat.
But though my other died . . .
I still won't let it sneak
and hide.
I love my hair
my mum knows how much I care.
My bedroom got decorated
the other week
every day I appreciate how
it is clean and neat.
My iPod is so cool
let's hope I don't drop it
in the pool!
All that falls into my life
let's hope I don't ruin it
with a knife!

Emma Seage (14)
Immanuel CE Community College, Idle

Friends

Friends are great,
Don't have hate,
They are the best,
Treat them like the rest.

Family is sharing,
They are so caring,
They treat you good,
As family should.

They're there when you need them,
They're there when you don't
But either way
They won't stay away.

Friends are great,
Don't have hate,
They are the best,
Don't put them to the test.

Family is sharing,
They are so caring,
They treat you good,
As family should.

Chrissie Aimee Doyle (13)
Immanuel CE Community College, Idle

Lion Poem

The lion is called Leo
He loves meat
He's brave and he is a sabre-tooth.

He could bite your head off in one bite
So never mess with Leo
He will take you down.

Richard Howard (11)
Immanuel CE Community College, Idle

My Family

I love my family,
I love my friends,
I like my friends,
They are funny!

I love me family,
They love me,
My dad,
He's a good cook!
My mum
Loves me,
I love her!

My sisters -
They are show-offs
My brothers -
They are good at drawing.

But most of all
I love
My dogs
Jacko.
Pepper.

Mykala Jackson (11)
Immanuel CE Community College, Idle

Friendship Matters To Me

What matters to me
Friendship matters to me!

Going out! Telling secrets
Always being there for you!
Helping you with everything.

Friendship is great
everybody has a best friend,
who they tell absolutely
everything to all the time
always having to mime,
when you can't talk,
that's best friends.

Friendship means a lot
friends are always kind to you
everybody has a best friend
who is always there to help them
and always there for you
when you need them.

Emily Hatfield (13)
Immanuel CE Community College, Idle

My Kitten

My kitten is nice to me
But sometimes he scratches me!

My kitten plays with me
He's soft and furry
Toulouse is his name.

He runs up the curtains
He's always doing that
But, he'll always have a home
My lovely furry cat.

Megan Cravan (11)
Immanuel CE Community College, Idle

Snow In Winter

The one thing I care about,
At this time of year,
Is playing out in the snow,
With my friends, right here!

You will know when,
Winter comes around,
Everything turns chilly,
And snowflakes come abound.

Lumps of snow perched precariously,
In fear of falling to their death,
This sight is enough,
To take away all breath.

A blanket of powdery snowflakes,
Settles on the ground,
All dancing gleefully,
But doesn't make a sound.

Sophie Coates (11)
Immanuel CE Community College, Idle

What Matters To Me

I like to start my day
By being clean and tidy.

By having my breakfast,
By getting dressed and brushing my teeth.

I like my pets.
I love my cat.
The dog is my best friend.

But the dog was cross.
And the cat went into the road.
It was killed because the car couldn't stop.

Kieran Exley (11)
Immanuel CE Community College, Idle

My Family

My family is important to me!

Mum's cooking rice
I have four sisters
Crystal, Joy, Chelsea, Jessica
And one brother.

Crystal has moved to York
And so has Joy too.

Jessica's the best
And Chelsea is the oldest.

David is my bro,
He's big and strong.

I love my family
And they love me!

Leon Blackburn (11)
Immanuel CE Community College, Idle

Love

There's no such thing as love.
Only if you love someone above.
There's no such thing as a relationship,
Because you say hello and end it by goodbye.
That's the worst thing that makes you cry.

It's just a waste of time and they always say, 'You're mine.'
Obviously not, when they only say, 'You're hot!'
And trying to give it a shot,
When at the end it just goes to pot!

You may get a rose and they may propose,
That to me is true love!
However there is such a thing as family love!
That to me matters!

Stephanie Tkatschuk (13)
Immanuel CE Community College, Idle

Love Catch

When you lose someone you love but they just fly away,
you try to recatch them day by day.

You never get closer you just become more apart,
but you know he is there deep in your heart.

As the wind blows it blows you more away,
like you're in a different time and a different day,
he will be going but you would just like to say.

He is the one, he will always be there,
no matter that I will always care
and he knows it from the love that we share.

This is not a game, no type of dare,
now all I've got to say is that I love you
and now that will forever and always stay.

Emma Payton (13)
Immanuel CE Community College, Idle

My Family

My mum
Makes me laugh!

My brother
Batters me for a joke!

My cat
Has sharp teeth!

My dog
Is really cute and fat!

RIP
Uncle Scott and
Nanna Sue
Who loved me more.

Kady Basson (12)
Immanuel CE Community College, Idle

What Matters To Me

What matters to me is my family
Mainly my little sister.
She makes me laugh.
What matters to me is my dad.
He is funny.
He playfights with me.
What matters to me is my mum.
Because she is the best.
She supports and listens to me.
What matters to me is Amy.
She is my big sister.
We always argue.
But we love each other lots.

Ellie-May Eastwood (11)
Immanuel CE Community College, Idle

My Special Book

I have a special book
I've had since I was one.
My mum used to read to me
When I was young.

Mum would always read it
But then one day it tore.
I was really mad with her as
We could read no more.

But then I got a new one
It came when I was three.
It was full of stories
Which my mum read to me.

Megan Fry Rodgers (11)
Immanuel CE Community College, Idle

Little Sister

I love . . .
my little sister because she's funny
and she likes to play with her toy bunny
she doesn't like honey

She sleeps like a cat
she is scared as a bat

My little sister likes to dress up
she can't do press-ups

My little sister is a bit clever
but she doesn't like bad weather.

Nicola Simpson (11)
Immanuel CE Community College, Idle

Special

My dog is special to me!
I chose him.
He's my dog.

My house is special to me!
I like it.
I helped to choose it.

My hamster is special to me!
Grayson is his name.
He bites me every morning!

Lizzie Amy Smith (12)
Immanuel CE Community College, Idle

My Dog

Every day I walk my dog
All over Idle moor
We come back in through the fog
Muddy paw prints on the floor

When we come back in
We like to have our tea
If we don't eat it, the leftovers go in the bin
If the dog could speak she'd probably say
'Hey you could've given that to me!'

Danny Shackleton (13)
Immanuel CE Community College, Idle

Autumn's Coming

When autumn comes the whole word changes,
The icy wind bites even the hearts of the warm-blooded creatures,
And the half-naked tree dances along.

The leaves have shed their old green coats
And now they're dressed in golden brown,
And conkers swing from the trees like an
Old knight's weapon, ready for the kill,
While helicopters spiral down like brown confetti at a wedding.

Fresh winter flowers are blooming in waves
Of pink, white and green.

Squirrels swarm and squabble over the last of the nuts to hide away,
Birds fly south in Vs, gliding on the evening breeze,
All the while the remaining birds are whistling along to tunes that only they know,
Waiting for the berries which are like chocolate to a child to them.

The sun rushes off earlier, late for an Australian summer beach party,
Leaving us in darkness, as autumn leaves and winter arrives.

Kathryn Bargh (12)
Queen Elizabeth's Grammar School, Horncastle

Autumn

Autumn breeze,
runs through the trees.
Birds are flying like an arrow head,
as they fly south to meet their winter bed.

Silent like a cat,
creeping up on its prey.
Pouncing on a rat
as it squeals in dismay.

Birds are whistling at their best,
whilst sitting in their nice, neat nest.
Leaves painted polka dot-brown,
others as gold as a king's crown.

Shorter days, longer nights,
people running between large lights.
Autumn is such an amazing sight,
even though the temperature has a nippy bite.

Nicole Gregory (12)
Queen Elizabeth's Grammar School, Horncastle

Autumn Is . . .

Misty mornings like steamed-up glass
A flock of birds flying past
Fires roaring on a cold night
Pumpkins with faces and haunting lights
Insects hovering above the icy cold ground
Animals sleeping, *sshhh!* Don't make a sound
Berries like baubles on a Christmas tree
Leaves that have fallen are now flying free
Polka dot patterned leaves crunching underfoot
The chimneys are filling up with soot
Twigs that point out like fingers on a hand
Pointing at the ploughed land.

Imogen Popham (12)
Queen Elizabeth's Grammar School, Horncastle

Autumn

Cold breeze in the early morning,
Squirrels collecting nuts,
Woodpeckers chattering on the wood,
As the wind whistles in the morning dew,
Crackle as the leaves disintegrate from footsteps,
Deserted there in a heap that the breeze abandoned,
Conkers, chestnuts on a nail floor,
Soon the ground will turn to mush.
The geese in bull horn-like file,
Migrating from the cold north,
Hibernation guarantees success,
As the animals get a good-earned rest,
The last day they rush around like bulls in a china shop.
Only hours till the end of autumn,
Brown fields in the dawning sun,
Trees unclad from autumn gold leaves,
Autumn ends on this chilling eve.

Nathan Poole (12)
Queen Elizabeth's Grammar School, Horncastle

Autumn

It is autumn,
The once living leaves leaving their old home,
To rest on the ground,
To then be trodden on and creak a loud, crisp sound,
The biting wind growling round near,
Disrupting the animals robbing food for next year,
Autumn is in full bloom,
Fresh fruit just right, I'd eat soon,
Now they are overdue,
Rotten and sour, their skin is hard as gel,
Birds from the south sing no more,
It is not autumn.

Emma Latchem (12)
Queen Elizabeth's Grammar School, Horncastle

Signs Of Autumn

The leaves are falling,
From the trees.
When conkers drop,
They break free.
The fields are being ploughed,
And look like a brown sea.
Squirrels hoard their nuts,
In an old tree.
Bushes start
To lose their berries
Fruit is bearing,
On the trees.
The harvest is going,
Fruitfully
Now winter's upon us!

Joseph Trevor (13)
Queen Elizabeth's Grammar School, Horncastle

Autumn

The autumn leaves
shed their smooth and
luxurious velvet coats to
show their crinkly, crispy
and crumbly skin.

As the leaves plummet to
their death the wind whistles
through the cold chilly air.

Although the leaves are dead
a sound repeats itself like
a rustling . . .
Autumn is still alive.

Jackson Draper (12)
Queen Elizabeth's Grammar School, Horncastle

Autumn

The nights were coming in like a massive army
converging on the world.

The blackberries were dying, as if the Grim Reaper walked past them and
ended their fruitful lives.

It was very cold, as if the Ice Age had returned and swept across the frozen
landscape.

The stricken trees were stripped of their leaves, as if a child's toys were
taken away.

The sun was sinking lower day by day, as if a weight pulled it towards the
dark frozen ground.

The conkers fell down from the sky like an artillery strike.

Bang! Autumn is dead. Winter's here.

Oliver Groombridge (13)
Queen Elizabeth's Grammar School, Horncastle

Oncoming Autumn

The fork-shaped leaves fall down the naked tree,
Slowly floating down to the soft, brown autumn ground.

The berries depart from their bushes as the animals gather a winter feast for
their hibernation.

The conkers, like smooth, silky stones clamber out of their green restricting
shells and hit the ground like grenades on a battlefield.

Birds are flying south, like remote-controlled homing missiles locked on
target of their destination of warmer weather.

The shortening days, closing in darkness on the world, the void slowly
moving over the sky, its spread increasing daily.

Joshua Evison (13)
Queen Elizabeth's Grammar School, Horncastle

Autumn Day

Moulting another summer coat, the tree felt cold
As the whistling wind blew past the naked bark.
The dazzling birds sang the sweetest song
Tweeting as the morning broke.
The wonderful walks as the excellent leaves fell against the freezing floor as
cold as deep space.
The sensational sun finally sets
The scent of the burning bonfire came over the gloomy night
It was the end of another autumn day.

Glyn Bates [12]
Queen Elizabeth's Grammar School, Horncastle

Idiomatic Relationship

She said he had a chip on his shoulder
                    But I couldn't smell any salt or vinegar,
He said she was driving him up the wall
                    But I couldn't see any tyre tracks,
She said loving him was a piece of cake
                    But I couldn't see any crumbs,
He said they were both in the same boat
                    But I saw her standing on the shore,
She said he was having a field day
                    But I knew he was working in town,
He said he was going to give her a taste of her own medicine
                    But he didn't go to the chemist,
She said he was as high as a kite
                    But I could see his footprints in the snow,
He said she had asked to take a rain check
                    But it was sunny outside,
She said his idea was a flash in the pan
                    But I knew he hadn't been cooking,
He said she had broken his heart
                    No really - she had!

Callum Hutchinson [12]
Queen Elizabeth's High School, Gainsborough

Animals From A Child's Point Of View

A is for animals, which this poem is about
B is for bear, just muscle in fur
C is for cats, well, big cats are the best
D is for deer, majestic and strong
E is for elephant, XXL in man size
F is for frogs, we used to leap like them in the playground
G is for giraffe, the tallest of all
H is for hippo, hippopotomousecow as my grandad used to say
I is for iguana, always relate them with Darwin
J is for jumpin' spider, my favourite of the 8s
K is for koala, symbolic and cute
L is for llama, one once spat on my teacher
M is for monkey, macaques are so cool
N is for naked mole rat, my mum hates those
O is for octopus, we were all scared
P is for panda, cute yet huge
Q is for quail, I never did like their eggs
R is for rabbit, always a favourite with the girls
S is for snake, simple and slithery, or shark, a favourite with the boys
T is for tiger, power and elegance
U is for you, human beings and mankind
V is for voles, now my dad is the expert
W is for worm, at the bottom of the garden
X is for X-ray, what would vets do without it?
Y is for why not save them for the future?
Z is for zebra because there's no other.

And all you've just read is 100% the truth,
Whatever your age from your first till last tooth.

Archie Bird (13)
Queen Elizabeth's High School, Gainsborough

Our Hero In The Ranks

Rise Sir Jamie, our hero in the ranks
A fighter made immortal
Creating brilliance, as if by magic
You couldn't have done it by yourself
But no comrade could equal you
Or astound as you've done
For you are a God, at least for tonight

First you were on your own
A solo effort so great
Nobody could touch you
And no defence could stop you
As 8000 people rose and 2000 cried
The chants began, the faces ecstatic
Our hero in the ranks

The second was scrappy
As your leader Sir Brian
And your sniper Billy Sharp
Contribute to the effort
You fight for your place
And as Sir Billy breaks down the defence
You take your chance
A block and a stab
A win safely predicted
For our hero in the ranks

Now your name
Chanted by all
Could be written in gold
The way you've performed
Jamie, Jamie
Jamie, Jamie
Coppinger
Is sung by all
Our hero in the ranks

There have been setbacks
The fight has been hard
They've put one past you
And the doubt becomes clear

But you've kept your head up
And not nearly had your fill
So off you go hunting
The support begging for more
From our hero in the ranks

And now there's an opening
A place barely touched
When you get there
You pick the ammo up
A long shot, easily missed
But your weaponry's enough
It's easy for you
Our hero in the ranks

The cheers fill your ears
You fall to your knees
The spoils of war
Your trophy a ball
For this is football
And the pitch is your home
Our hero in the ranks.

Matthew Dryden (14)
Queen Elizabeth's High School, Gainsborough

Clique

Cheerleaders? Preps?
Athletes and jocks,
Geeks? Nerds?
Emos or goths

Cheerleaders cheering,
Arms are all linked.
Preps loudly gossiping,
Head to toe in pink.

The geeks and the nerds;
They're nearly the same.
But geeks are quite cool,
Nerds are just lame.

The ones that are sporty
Are put into lots,
The normals are athletes,
The coolest are jocks.

Next are the weirdos,
The emos and goths.
Goths are quite scary
And emos cry a lot.

Cheerleader or prep?
Athlete or jock?
Geek? Nerd?
Emo or goth?

Who do you belong to?

Alice Walton (13)
Queen Elizabeth's High School, Gainsborough

Seasons

It's seeing the newborn baby lambs,
It's discovering the blossom on the trees.
It's smelling the fresh mornings,
And new beginnings . . .
It must be spring . . .

It's feeling the blazing sun on your back,
It's seeing the morning dew.
It's savouring the taste of BBQs
And refreshing iced drinks too . . .
It must be summer . . .

It's seeing the oranges of all the trees,
It's sensing the leaves crunch under your feet.
It's catching a whiff of the bonfire,
And hearing fireworks at night . . .
It must be autumn . . .

It's opening the curtains and seeing white,
It's the smell of mulled wine wafting through the air.
It's feeling the cold of the snow in your hands,
And seeing everyone's happy faces on Christmas Day
It must be winter . . .

It's spring, it's summer.
It's autumn, it's winter.
It's love shown in four different ways,
Beautiful in them all . . .
It is the seasons . . .

Emma Barker (13)
Queen Elizabeth's High School, Gainsborough

Nature Is Everything

Nature is everywhere,
Nature is here,
Inside and outside,
Outside and in.

Nature can be good,
Like when the flowers begin to bud
But nature can be bad,
Like when the ice begins to crack . . .
And I fall down and hurt my back!

Nature is everything,
Nature is here,
Inside and outside,
Outside and in.

Nature is colourful,
So naturally beautiful,
Reds, blues, greens and pinks,
Standing out against this concrete world that has evolved,
So eager and desperate to be involved.

Nature is so difficult to define,
But nature is everywhere,
Nature is here,
Nature is everything,
And that's just fine.

Emma-Louise Bratley (14)
Queen Elizabeth's High School, Gainsborough

You Are To Me

You are to me . . .
Mascara, you open up my eyes.
A pair of heels, you give me a lift.
A heartbeat, constantly reassuring me.
A best friend, you know just what to say.
You are to me . . .
Martin Luther King, you dare to dream.
A fire, constantly warming my heart.
Like the sun, you lighten up my day.
You are to me . . .
A key to unlock doors to new possibilities.
A hair grip, you keep everything in place.
An umbrella, you protect me in all kinds of weather.
You are to me . . .
A coat, you keep me warm in rain or storm.
A photograph, you make old memories come to life.
A teddy bear, you're always there for a cuddle.
You are to me . . .
A flag, proud of who you are.
A flower, a beauty on its own.
A shooting star, you give me hope and wishes too.
But best of all you are to me . . .
A dream come true!

Marietta Hahn (12)
Queen Elizabeth's High School, Gainsborough

Poor People

There are poor people all over the world.
People ignore them and just walk past saying
it's their fault they got there.
Poor people praying for one night of warmth.
Please don't ignore them because one day
you might be begging for stuff to eat.
Think about the poor people sleeping on the street.
Think about the poor people without enough to eat.

They sleep in a box.
You sleep in a house, in a nice warm house.
Two pounds is nothing to you, but to them it could buy some food.
They carry their things in carrier bags.
The things they stole just to get by.
Think about the poor people sleeping on the street.
Think about the poor people without enough to eat.

So next time you're rustling by.
Stop, think.
Say hello, give some money, a friendly face
or as little as toothpaste.
It's worth it when you see them walk off with an ear to ear grin.
Think about the poor people sleeping on the street.
Think about the poor people without enough to eat.

Kieran O'Donoghue (13)
Queen Elizabeth's High School, Gainsborough

A Day In The Snow

I went to Zoë's
It was snowing
We went on the sledge
And fell off the edge

We had a great laugh
In the freezing cold
We built a snowman
And named it Dan!

An hour later
We had a snowball fight
Which of course, I won!
Then we went in and had an ice bun!

We sat by the fire
And drank hot chocolate
Yum, yum, yum!
My belly started to run!

We went back out
And we built an igloo
In our coats, scarves and gloves
Then out came her mum
And said that was the end of our fun!

Heather Pettit (13)
Queen Elizabeth's High School, Gainsborough

My Dog

My dog is amazing,
She doesn't like anything louder than a 'ting'
My dog is called Tia,
She will come if you shout 'here'

My dog is black and white,
And if she runs, in seconds she's out of sight,
She has a cute pink nose,
And is scared of our garden hose.

My dog is fast,
She runs like lightning, and you never see her go past,
She wakes us all up, when she runs upstairs,
But no one really cares.

My dog likes curry,
She likes to be in the way, when you're in a hurry.
She's been to the beach,
We put her on a surfboard, and tried to teach.

My dog loves me,
And I love her more than chocolate by Cadbury.
She has lovely fur,
And I can't imagine life without her.

Zoë Hanoman (14)
Queen Elizabeth's High School, Gainsborough

That Black Cat

I only once saw that black cat,
Running swiftly down the road,
The moon itself looked down with fear,
Crying as it glowed.

The cats' noise was nil,
Hiding in midnight shadows,
Waiting for the kill.

A small mouse ran by,
Scampering freely with joy,
Spied cat, let out cry.

The black cat lunged,
What a glorious sight,
Sleek fur glistening, claws outstretched,
Ready for a fight.

I only once saw that black cat,
Carrying its prize down the road,
The moon itself looked down with fear,
Crying as it glowed.

Ryan Morris (13)
Queen Elizabeth's High School, Gainsborough

Me And My Friends

My friends are quite an odd bunch, variety here, variety there
First comes Mole, funny to the end
Even when I want the end to come soon
Next is the smartie, a lot smarter, smaller, sillier than me.
Sometimes I wonder maybe he's a calculator:
Then there's Veggie, the funniest moment is when
she screamed at some chicken!
Fourth comes Toph, well how can you describe him
apart from a little weird?
After him is the rebel.
His personality is a lot bigger than his size of 3 foot 2.
Next is T who everybody likes.
I'm surprised people aren't put off by the amount he farts!
Then there is Lucky, though not in love.
He's so beautifully besotted, it makes me wanna spew!

Well that's all in my close circle.
I could go into detail, give you the inside scoop,
but then I'd be dead and for some rather odd reason,
I quite like my head!

George Andrews (13)
Queen Elizabeth's High School, Gainsborough

Under The Street Lamp

I ran down the alley.
With you close behind.
I sprinted a bit,
But you were faster.
You caught me up and tackled me.
I lay on the floor,
And tried to catch my breath.
You looked into my eyes,
Then stood and grabbed my hand.
You pulled me up,
And, hand in hand,
We walked away.
Under the light of the streetlamp,
You pulled me close and kissed me.
I woke with a start.
It was only a dream,
But how I wish it were true.

Jasmine Louise Burrows (13)
Queen Elizabeth's High School, Gainsborough

Through My Eyes

Through my eyes I see a world filled with distress and pain,
From devastating floods to Florida's last hurricane.

Through my eyes I see orphans living in slums and a lonely child starved to death.

Through my eyes I see helpless people fighting for their say,
Yet the fortunate ones complain of low pay.

Through my eyes I see that one hard-working nurse,
Helping out the poor but with no money left in her purse.

Through my eyes I see thousands of campaigners trying to give,
Doing all in their power to make sure others live.

Through my eyes I see some of my classmates.
Too worried about themselves and who Jordan now hates.

We all need to open our eyes and take a clear look around.

Be grateful for what we have - running water, hot food and the television's sound.

Jessica Bedward (12)
Queen Elizabeth's High School, Gainsborough

Scunthorpe

S unny Scunny get real
C an't be sunny in England
U nited beat our footy skills
N ext time we'll win
T hat you can be sure
H olidays spent at the cinema
O r at the leisure centre
R ight up your bowling alley
P erhaps a little shopping
E ven to a car boot sale
　 Anything but back to school!

Scott Curtis (14)
Queen Elizabeth's High School, Gainsborough

Enjoy Life!

Remember when you were young and striving,
When you worked hard and always tried,
Then you turned to the wrong sort of people,
And soon you were on alcohol, crack and fights.

When you started it just got worse,
Cheating on tests at school and at work,
You lied, you cheated and you hurt other people,
You had changed into one of those gang people.

Remember when you were a grade A druggy
Remember when you lied,
Remember when you cheated,
And all those other things you shouldn't have tried.

So turn back time to change the things you did,
And this time say, 'No!' and don't get started with it,
Just remember when you loved and always tried,
And just one more thing, enjoy life!

Antonia Barber (12)
Queen Elizabeth's High School, Gainsborough

The Lilac Room

I stepped through the portal, to the lilac room.
I wondered where we'd end up today.
Maybe we'd travel on a pirate ship to the notorious Pegleg Bay!
Or we might visit Wonderland and see the late white bunny!
Or hold up a bank and steal jewels and money!
We could journey on horseback to the wild Wild West.
Or dive down to the bottom of the sea and find the magic chest!
Anything from Pegleg Bay to a white bunny to lots of money, the Wild West
to a magic chest.
It all happens in the lilac room.
The lilac room.
The English room.

Lindsey Brooks (12)
Queen Elizabeth's High School, Gainsborough

Cheetah Or Cheater?

As slimline as a flipping fast F1 car,
As slick as a mean, cheeky monkey,
As fast as a bright bold light,
As sly as a sad, dirty thief,

The speed of a silly, silent sound,
The cunning of a slick, tricky businessman,
The elegance of the posh, perky Queen,
The deceitfulness of a wicked, evil trickster,

The endangered,
The surplus,
The lovely,
The cruel,

The fragile cheetah,
The deceptive cheater.

Sam Johnson (12)
Queen Elizabeth's High School, Gainsborough

The Match

Preparations were in place,
Opposing teams meet face to face.
Anticipation starts to rise,
One team will meet its demise.
The ref's whistle screamed, 'Start!'
And so did the tempting food cart.
The ball is passed from feet to feet,
Controlled and kicked in the blazing heat.
Surely bound for a goal,
Spectators tense as it hits the pole.
Eager player takes a corner kick,
Peter Crouch provides the flick.
Excited roars shake through the crowd,
Supporting fans are ever so proud.

James Rayner (12)
Queen Elizabeth's High School, Gainsborough

Ellie-Mae

Everyone is E xcited from the birth
They named her E L lie-Mae
Her tiny, little L egs kicking about
Wh I lst everyone is gathering
H E r laugh is the cutest thing
It's been six M onths now
And she can A lmost crawl
My beautiful ni E ce Ellie-Mae!

Lauren Green (13)
Queen Elizabeth's High School, Gainsborough

Life Is Like . . .

Life is like a maze
Finding the start
Never the end.

Life is like a dream
Everything going right
But it's too good to be true.

Life is like an essay
So hard
So many words.

Life is like a roller coaster
It's up
And it's down
But eventually . . .
You get off!

Kai Benson (12)
Queen Elizabeth's High School, Gainsborough

Annoyed

It really annoys me when . . .
Your coffee goes cold
When you only have an odd pair of socks
When your paper won't neatly fold
It really annoys me when . . .
Cows are brown
When rubber ducks aren't yellow
When the Queen doesn't wear a crown
It really annoys me when . . .
Someone in front of you randomly stops
When sheep are shorn
When fireworks have no bangs or pops
It really annoys me when . . .

You can't find anything to end a poem!

Phoebe Gillian Hoar (12)
Queen Elizabeth's High School, Gainsborough

The Body

He looked almost the same
As he did the last time
I saw him, with his peachy skin
And deep brown eyes.

He lay there, lifeless
And it sent a shiver
Down my spine.
I touched his face
And it was ice-cold.

He left
A hole in my heart
Like they did
When they left him
In a pool of blood.

Charlie Rodgers (14)
Rawmarsh Comprehensive School, Rawmarsh

Featured Poets:
DEAD POETS
AKA Mark Grist & MC Mixy

Mark Grist and MC Mixy joined forces to become the 'Dead Poets' in 2008.

Since then Mark and Mixy have been challenging the preconceptions of poetry and hip hop across the country. As 'Dead Poets', they have performed in venues ranging from nightclubs to secondary schools; from festivals to formal dinners. They've appeared on Radio 6 Live with Steve Merchant, they've been on a national tour with Phrased and Confused and debuted their show at the 2010 Edinburgh Fringe, which was a huge success.

Both Mark and Mixy work on solo projects as well as working together as the 'Dead Poets'. Both have been Peterborough's Poet Laureate, with Mixy holding the title for 2010.

The 'Dead Poets' are available for workshops in your school as well as other events. Visit www.deadpoetry.co.uk for further information and to contact the guys!

Read on to pick up some fab writing tips!

Your WORKSHOPS

In these workshops we are going to look at writing styles and examine some literary techniques that the 'dead poets' use. Grab a pen, and let's go!

Rhythm Workshop

Rhythm in writing is like the beat in music. Rhythm is when certain words are produced more forcefully than others, and may be held for longer duration. The repetition of a pattern is what produces a 'rhythmic effect'. The word rhythm comes from the Greek meaning of 'measured motion'.

Count the number of syllables in your name. Then count the number of syllables in the following line, which you write in your notepad: 'My horse, my horse, will not eat grass'.

Now, highlight the longer sounding syllables and then the shorter sounding syllables in a different colour.

Di dum, di dum, di dum, di dum is a good way of summing this up.

You should then try to write your own lines that match this rhythm. You have one minute to see how many you can write!

Examples include:
'My cheese smells bad because it's hot'
and
'I do not like to write in rhyme'.

For your poem, why don't you try to play with the rhythm? Use only longer beats or shorter beats? Create your own beat and write your lines to this?

Did you know ... ?

Did you know that paper was invented in China around 105AD by Ts'ai Lun. The first English paper mill didn't open until 1590 and was in Dartford.

Rhyme Workshop

Start off with the phrase 'I'd rather be silver than gold' in your notepad. and see if you can come up with lines that rhyme with it -
'I'd rather have hair than be bald'
'I'd rather be young than be old'
'I'd rather be hot than cold'
'I'd rather be bought than sold'

Also, pick one of these words and see how many rhymes you can find:

Rose

Wall

Warm

Danger

What kinds of rhymes did you come up with? Are there differences in rhymes? Do some words rhyme more cleanly than others? Which do you prefer and why?

Onomatopoeia Workshop

Divide a sheet of A4 paper into 8 squares.

You then have thirty seconds to draw/write what could make the following sounds:

Splash	Ping
Drip	Bang
Rip	Croak
Crack	Splash

Now try writing your own ideas of onomatopoeia. Why might a writer include onomatopoeia in their writing?

Lists Workshop

Game - you (and you can ask your friends or family too) to write as many reasons as possible for the following topics:

Annoying things about siblings

The worst pets ever

The most disgusting ingredients for a soup you can think of

Why not try writing a poem with the same first 2, 3 or 4 words?

I am ...

Or

I love it when ...

Eg:

I am a brother

I am a listener

I am a collector of secrets

I am a messer of bedrooms.

Repetition Workshop

Come up with a list of words/phrases, aim for at least 5. You now must include one of these words in your piece at least 6 times. You aren't allowed to place these words/phrases at the beginning of any of the lines.

Suggested words/phrases:

Why

Freedom

Laughing

That was the best day ever

I can't find the door

I'm in trouble again

The best

Workshop
POETRY 101

Below is a poem written especially for Poetry Matters, by MC Mixy. Why not try and write some more poems of your own?

What is Matter?

© MC Mixy

What matters to me may not be the same things that matter to you
You may not agree with my opinion mentality or attitude
The order in which I line up my priorities to move
Choose to include my view and do what I do due to my mood
And state of mind
I make the time to place the lines on stacks of paper and binds
Concentrate on my artwork hard I can't just pass and scrape behind
Always keep close mates of mine that make things right
And even those who can't … just cos I love the way they can try
What matters to me is doing things the right way
It's tough this game of life we play what we think might stray from what others might say
In this world of individuality we all wanna bring originality
Live life and drift through casually but the vicious reality is
Creativity is unique
Opinions will always differ but if you figure you know the truth, speak
So many things matter to me depending on how tragically deep you wanna go
I know I need to defy gravity on this balance beam
As I laugh and breathe draft and read map the scene practise piece smash the beat and graphic release
Visual and vocal it's a standard procedure
Have to believe and don't bite the hand when it feeds ya

If you wanna be a leader you need to stay out of the pen where the sheep
are
The things that matter to me are
My art and my friends
That will stay from the start to the end
People will do things you find hard to amend
Expect the attacks and prepare you gotta be smart to defend
I put my whole heart in the blend the mass is halved yet again
I'm marked by my pen a big fish fighting sharks of men
In a small pond
Dodging harpoons and nets hooks and predators tryna dismember ya
I won't let them I won't get disheartened I can fend for myself
As long as I'm doing what's important
I'm my mind where I'm supported is a just cause to be supporting
In these appalling hard times I often find myself falling when
Only two aspects of my life keep me sane and allow me to stand tall again
Out of all of them two is a small number
It's a reminder I remind ya to hold necessity and let luxury fall under
Try to avoid letting depression seep through
Take the lesson we actually need a lot less than we think we do
So what matters to you?
They may be similar to things that matter to me
I'm actually lacking the need of things I feel would help me to succeed
Though I like to keep it simple, I wanna love, I wanna breed
I'm one of many individuals in this world where importance fluctuates and
varies
Things that matter will come and go
But the ones that stay for long enough must be worth keeping close
If you're not sure now don't watch it you'll know when you need to know
Me, I think I know now … yet I feel and fear I don't.

Turn overleaf for a poem by Mark Grist
and some fantastic hints and tips!

Workshop
POETRY 101

What Tie Should I Wear Today?

© Mark Grist

I wish I had a tie that was suave and silk and slick,
One with flair, that's debonair and would enchant with just one flick,
Yeah, I'd like that … a tie that's hypnotizing,
I'd be very restrained and avoid womanising,
But all the lady teachers would still say 'Mr Grist your tie's so charming!'
As I cruise into their classrooms with it striking and disarming.
At parents' evenings my tie's charm would suffice,
In getting mums to whisper as they leave 'Your English teacher seems nice!'

Or maybe an evil-looking tie - one that's the business,
Where students will go 'Watch out! Mr Grist is
on the prowl with that evil tie.'
The one that cornered Josh and then ripped out his eye.
Yeah no one ever whispers, no one ever sniggers,
Or my tie would rear up and you'd wet your knickers.
Maybe one girl just hasn't heard the warning,
Cos she overslept and turned up late to school that morning,
And so I'd catch her in my lesson yawning … oh dear.
I'd try to calm it down, but this tie's got bad ideas.
It'd size the girl up and then just as she fears,
Dive in like a serpent snapping at her ears.
There'd be a scream, some blood and lots and lots of tears,
And she wouldn't be able to yawn again for years.

Or maybe … a tie that everyone agrees is mighty fine
And people travel from miles around to gawp at the design
I'd like that … a tie that pushes the boundaries of tieware right up to the limit
It'd make emos wipe their tears away while chavs say 'It's wicked innit?'
and footy lads would stop me with 'I'd wear that if I ever won the cup.'
And I'd walk through Peterborough to slapped backs, high fives, thumbs up
While monosyllabic teenagers would just stand there going 'Yup.'

I don't know. I'd never be sure which of the three to try
As any decision between them would always end a tie.

Tips and Advice for PERFORMING Your Poem

So you've written your poem, now how about performing it.
Whether you read your poem for the first time in front of your class, school
or strangers at an open mic event or poetry slam, these tips will help you
make the best of your performance.

Breathe and try to relax.

Every poet that reads in front of people for the first time feels a bit nervous,
when you're there you are in charge and nothing serious can go wrong.

People at poetry slams or readings are there to support the poets. They really are!

If you can learn your poem off by heart that is brilliant, however having a piece of paper or notebook with your work in is fine, though try not to hide behind these.

It's better to get some eye contact with the audience.
If you're nervous find a friendly face to focus on.

Try to read slowly and clearly and enjoy your time in the spotlight.

Don't rush up to the microphone, make sure it's at the right height for you and if you need it adjusted ask one of the team around you.

Before you start, stand up as straight as you can and get your body as
comfortable as you can and remember to hold your head up.

The microphone can only amplify what what's spoken into it; if you're very loud you might
end up deafening people and if you only whisper or stand too far away you won't be heard.

When you say something before your poem, whether that's hello or just the title of your poem, try and have a listen to how loud you sound. If you're too quiet move closer to the microphone, if you're too loud move back a bit.

Remember to breathe! Don't try to say your poem so quickly you can't find
time to catch your breath.

And finally, **enjoy!**

Poetry FACTS

Here are a selection of fascinating poetry facts!

No word in the English language rhymes with 'MONTH'.

William Shakespeare was born on 23rd April 1564 and died on 23rd April 1616.

The haiku is one of the shortest forms of poetic writing.
Originating in Japan, a haiku poem is only seventeen syllables, typically broken down into three lines of five, seven and five syllables respectively.

**The motto of the Globe Theatre was 'totus mundus agit histrionem'
(the whole world is a playhouse).**

The Children's Laureate award was an idea by Ted Hughes and Michael Morpurgo.

The 25th January each year is Burns' Night, an occasion in honour of Scotland's national poet Robert Burns.

Spike Milligan's 'On the Ning Nang Nong' was voted the UK's favourite comic poem in 1998.

Did you know *onomatopoeia* means the word you use sounds like the word you are describing – like the rain *pitter-patters* or the snow *crunches* under my foot.

'Go' is the shortest complete sentence in the English language.

**Did you know rhymes were used in olden days to help people remember the news?
Ring-o'-roses is about the Plague!**

The Nursery Rhyme 'Old King Cole' is based on a real king and a real historical event. King Cole is supposed to have been an actual monarch of Britain who ruled around 200 A.D.

Edward Lear popularised the limerick with his poem 'The Owl and the Pussy-Cat'.

Lewis Carroll's poem 'The Jabberwocky' is written in nonsense style.

POEM – noun

1. a composition in verse, esp. one that is characterized by a highly developed artistic form and by the use of heightened language and rhythm to express an intensely imaginative interpretation of the subject.

Poetry TIPS

We have compiled some helpful tips for you budding poets...

In order to write poetry, read lots of poetry!

Keep a notebook with you at all times so you can write whenever (and wherever) inspiration strikes.

Every line of a poem should be important to the poem and interesting to read. A poem with only 3 great lines should be 3 lines long.

Use an online rhyming dictionary to improve your vocabulary.

Use free workshops and help sheets to learn new poetry styles.

Experiment with visual patterns - does your written poetry create a good pattern on the page?

Try to create pictures in the reader's mind - aim to fire the imagination.

Develop your voice. Become comfortable with how you write.

Listen to criticism, and try to learn from it, but don't live or die by it.

Say what you want to say, let the reader decide what it means.

Notice what makes other's poetry memorable. Capture it, mix it up and make it your own. (Don't copy other's work word for word!)

Go wild. Be funny. Be serious. Be whatever you want!

Grab hold of something you feel - anything you feel - and write it.

The more you write, the more you develop. Write poetry often.

Use your imagination, your own way of seeing.

Feel free to write a bad poem, it will develop your 'voice'.

Did you know ...?

'The Epic of Gilgamesh' was written thousands of years ago in Mesopotamia and is the oldest poem on record.

Wordsmith

The *premier* magazine
for creative young people

A platform for your imagination and creativity. Showcase your ideas and have your say. Welcome to a place where like-minded young people express their personalities and individuality knows no limits.

For further information visit ***www.youngwriters.co.uk***.

A peek into Wordsmith world ...

Poetry and Short Stories

We feature both themed and non-themed work every issue. Previous themes have included; dreams and aspirations, superhero stories and ghostly tales.

Next Generation Author

This section devotes two whole pages to one of our readers' work. The perfect place to showcase a selection of your poems, stories or both!

Guest Author, Workshops & Features

Interesting and informative tutorials on different styles of poetry and creative writing. Famous authors and illustrators share their advice with us on how to create gripping stories and magical picturebooks. Novelists like Michael Morpurgo and Celia Rees go under the spotlight to answer our questions.

The fun doesn't stop there ...

Every issue we tell you what events are coming up
across the country. We keep you up to date with the latest film and book releases and we feature some yummy recipes to help feed the brain and get the creative juices flowing.

So with all this and more, Wordsmith is *the* magazine to be reading.

If you are too young for Wordsmith magazine or have a younger friend who enjoys creative writing, then check out Scribbler!. Scribbler! is for 7-11 year-olds and is jam-packed full of brilliant features, young writers' work, competitions and interviews too. For further information check out ***www.youngwriters.co.uk*** or ask an adult to call us on (01733) 890066.

To get an adult to subscribe to either magazine for you,
ask them to visit the website or give us a call.

Be Proud

Trailing along the desert,
Sun shining seductively,
Our brave soldiers protecting me,

One by one,
They follow on.

Back home we support,
For those who have fought,
Remembering those who did not return.

One by one
They follow on.

The enduring days they steadily pace,
Engaging the enemy face-to-face,

One by one
They follow on.

We are all proud
Of these men and women
Who serve our country
In times of war.

The fallen continue to live
Through our memories.

One by one
They follow on.

Alex Southall (14)
Rawmarsh Comprehensive School, Rawmarsh

What Matters To Me

What matters to me
is friends and family
even though they annoy me
I need them
like oxygen
if I lost them
my world would crash!
They've mattered since dawn
or when I was born
I wouldn't live without them

COD is best of all
every gun I have fall
'tac nukes' I call
I always play free for all
I own all

What I also like
is riding my bike
pulling a wheelie
just like 'Steelie'
BMX on the ramps
pictures airing lamps
gap over Scout camps
I am the champ

Backflips, front flips
side flips, all
no fear I have, I just don't think at all.
But the sad thing is
it's all in my head
I really own all
because I don't fall
at a sport called skiing

I am Bristish champ
double blackflip some ramps
540, 720, 900, 1080
whatever's ahead
I put it to bed
'Wow' is all I hear
but it is quite clear
I'm lying, oh dear!

Tyler Harding (14)
Ryburn Valley High School, Sowerby

What Matters To Me

What matters to me is that my friends and family will stick by me
Mum and Dad will love me
Sister will beat me but will still love me
Dad will work
Mum will cook
What matters to me
Simply has to be
With my dad
Having a laugh
Kicking a ball
What matters to me are my sports
Playing rugby on a field,
In the boxing ring, people hitting me
That is what matters to me.
Mum and Dad very lazy,
Sister so crazy
School is so boring sitting in a chair
That is what matters to me
Money in the pocket watching rubbish
Hockey on the big TV
Having lots of fun
After eating a creamy bun.

Jack Matthews (13)
Ryburn Valley High School, Sowerby

What Matters To Me

School what can I say?
Well I'm there nearly every day,
It can be boring but also fun
You get a lot of homework and it weighs a ton,

School matters to me because
Though it's not that cool,
If you don't go later in life
You feel a fool,

Detentions are not that fun,
You feel like you want to run,
PE can be great,
As long as you're not late,

Breaktime is exciting
You don't have to do any writing,
Our uniform is not that nice,
They need to get some serious advice,

School matters to me because
I need the grades,
Maths is alright
That's only because I'm bright,

Tec is fantastic, you get to
Mess with plastic
Assembly is always a drag
When it's over I wave a flag,

School matters to me because,
I will be able to have a good future
And so I can get a good career.

Sophie Cox (12)
Ryburn Valley High School, Sowerby

What Matters To Me?

My mates are a laugh
they are the best
My mates really care
they do yes

My mates are a laugh
they are always hyper
trying to steal my shoes
and helping me all the time

My family they care
there's my dad
he's a plumber
and my mum
she's a cook
There's my bro Jordan
He's so annoying
and my other brother Dean
Who's actually OK.

They always care
They're always there
but they don't share
I couldn't be happier with them.

There's:
Ellie, she's crazy
Jenna, she's awesome
Georgia, she's hyper
Charli, she's mad
Simon, he's odd
Gemma, she's bad . . . not
Reece, he's well . . .
Sandra, she's lol
Shannon, she's shy
that's just about it, well
except for me.

Zoe Kerridge (12)
Ryburn Valley High School, Sowerby

What Matters To Me

What matters to me
Simply has to be
My kind and loving friends
Who will be there till the end
They are always smiling and happy
Even if I'm a little snappy

Sometimes I think they're rather strange
But I hope that will never change
When I am upset and down
They will be trying to make me happy by being a clown
We have a laugh
We have a chat
We have a ball
When we need to talk we just call
And say, 'That was a tough day.'

One day I said to my friend, 'Come and meet my mum,'
Then I realised that was quite dumb
My family are so crazy
My brothers very lazy
My dad tells bad jokes
But they're friendly to other folk

I have many pets as well
They sometimes really smell
My dog is happy and full of life
After a bone from a butcher's knife
So I think that my family and friends
Matter to me and over all
I am as happy as can be.

Emma Walton (13)
Ryburn Valley High School, Sowerby

What Matters To Me

What matters to me
It's the key
The cold silver against my neck
Circles and stars
The protection of amazing angels
Evil's got no chance

A pentagram is what it is
I wear it on my finger
In hope that danger doesn't linger
It's always with me
Wherever I go
To keep hope that I don't get sent below

This symbol is from 1835
And I'm just keeping the superstition alive
The wedding finger of my left hand
That is where it will stay

The pentagram is my bodyguard
It's for protection against devils
It makes me feel safe on so many levels
I will never find a demon in my safest haven.

I drew it on my door
It's like my law
In my own little bubble
I'm always in enclosed arms
No one can get to me now
And that's what matters to me . . .

Rebecca Crossley (13)
Ryburn Valley High School, Sowerby

What Matters To Me

What matters to me,
Well there's family and friends, dancing too,
I do ballroom and Latin, there's sequence too.
Dancing I do with all my friends,
Dancing and prancing until the day ends.
Now when it comes to friends what can I say?
We tell secrets, have a laugh and help each other through the day.
Friends at school, friends at home,
They stay with you, wherever you go.
Family, family, family,
This one's a little harder.
We go to the seaside,
Care about each other,
We have massive parties for birthdays and Christmas
Yeah, my family's like no other
Families stick by you whatever you do,
Through the good and the bad times,
And when you're feeling blue.
There's one more thing that matters to me
That's my little rabbit, Fudge,
That is special you see,
She's my first ever pet and I love her so much,
She lives in our cellar, in her untidy hutch
So there we are, what matters to me,
In just a few short lines,
I love every single one of these things,
And they stay with me all the time.

Sophie Norburn (13)
Ryburn Valley High School, Sowerby

What Matters To Me?

The friends and family
Are everything to me
If I didn't have them
I don't know where I would be.
My mother and father
Brother and all
Without them around
I would clearly just fall.
Sometimes they're unfaithful
Laugh when times get hard
But I know they are always there
Every moment we share
They stick by me
Through thick and thin
We have our good times
We even go dancing.
They are people I can count on
Everything I hoped they would be
They are there, for every care
They are there, for every tear
I wouldn't let them go
Because oh I love them so
I have to remember
People change
Things go wrong
But I have to remember that life goes on.

Jessica Martin (13)
Ryburn Valley High School, Sowerby

What Matters To Me

What matters to me
What matters to me

What matters to me is my family.

My dad works away
And my mum stays at home
She's so much like a phone
When I ring she comes on
Hand and foot.

My dog is my friend
I play with her all the time
I get her things
Is that such a crime?

My auntie and uncle
They're so nice
They let me
Sleep sometimes
It's right next to school
And that's a pain.

My grandma and grandad
Are very nice
They give me money
And lots of spice.

Simon Valentine (12)
Ryburn Valley High School, Sowerby

What Matters To Me

I like football
I watch it every day.
I love football
It's what I always play.
I support Liverpool FC
They make me so jolly.

I tie my boots at nine in the morning
No wonder I'm always yawning
I love my boot
It helps me when I shoot.

I play in mid or defence
My team is so immense
We don't really work as a team
That's why our captain always screams.
But we throw losing in the bin
And always have to win.

Even when we lose we will always stand tall.
What matters to me,
Is my football.

Ben Widdop (12)
Ryburn Valley High School, Sowerby

Football Poem

What matters to me is,
Football,
Football's great,
Football's my life,
Football's my thing,
I support Liverpool FC,
I play for Halifax Irish,
And we've only lost one game,
Football rocks,
Football, I shoot, I try to score,
Football is awesome to me,
And I never back down,
And I will never quit,
And I will never stop running,
Although this poem doesn't rhyme
Football matters to me,
It's so great, I play all the time,
Football matters to me,
And nothing else does matter to me.

James McIntyre (12)
Ryburn Valley High School, Sowerby

The Straight Life

What matters to me, won't matter to you.
Are you ready? Let's go. Let's go.

I have these things that heat up quick,
My sizzling straighteners are hot and slick,
As they make my hair all styled and straight,
A smile appears, oh yeah but wait.

A f-l-i-c to the k decides to come and raid my hair,
Before I leave and go to school,
I need to get rid of this crazy fool
Flick, flick, flick, it's getting worse
I must have some kinda hair curse.

While I stress and straighten my hair
My flicks just go and I'm happy again
Does it matter to you? Cos it matters to me.

The straight life.

Hannah Stead (13)
Ryburn Valley High School, Sowerby

What Matters To Me

Chocolate and crisps, I could eat them all day,
Friends are there always to stay.

When I get in I'm straight on the netbook,
I love my clothes and shopping in New Look.

My family are there to help and care for me,
My kittens are cute as my baby sister, they're so cuddly.

Swimming is fun especially with friends,
I love going on the slides and going round the bends.

What I like best is hanging out with my mates,
We have the best sleepovers cos we stay up late.

Also I love chatting the most as well,
But please can you not tell!

Finally I love going on my mobile phone and texting to people all the time,
This is the end of my little rhyme.

I've written too much about 'what matters to me'.

Ellie Coyle (14)
Ryburn Valley High School, Sowerby

Best Friends

B est friends are like family, they stay together and help you
E verlasting love . . .
S tay together forever
T he crew hang together

F orever and always, always and forever
R ing is a circle, it has no end like friendship
I love them
E ndless friendship
N ever dies or ever goes
D aydream with them
S tay with them!

Phoebe Cretney (12)
Ryburn Valley High School, Sowerby

What Matters To Me

Every life has a starting gate
like every fisherman has bait
everyone is waiting for the gate to drop
we have our ups and downs
like uphill and downhill jumps
Sometimes you crash and burn and don't get back up
in this race you're trying to beat everyone
to get to the top
but sometimes you drop
from motocross to moaning, rapping to screaming
parents can be annoying
parents are like gods, they watch over you
even though they may sound like poo
but they support you in everything you do
even if you lose
that's what matters to me.

Doltan Shannon (13)
Ryburn Valley High School, Sowerby

What Matters To Me

What matters to me is my family
That's why I am a loving human being . . .
What matters to me are my pets
That's why I go to the vet's
What matters to me are my models
That's why I go to the model shops
What matters to me are my friends and B-friends
That's why I am popular
What matters to me are planes
That's why I look to the sky
What matters to me are my laptop and TV
That's why I know a lot
What matters to me is my future.

Reece Callum Hutton (13)
Ryburn Valley High School, Sowerby

What Matters To Me?

What matters to me
Is my pets
My fish from the sea
With their bridge and fishing nets.

What matters to me
Is my sport
It doesn't matter if it's rugby or skiing
Or even tennis on the courts.

What matters to me
Is my family
We live together in harmony
All my family likes me.

What matters to me
Is my TV
I always watch ITV3
This is what matters to me.

Jack Bruce (12)
Ryburn Valley High School, Sowerby

What Matters To Me?

What matters to me is winter
the winter is cold
it comes and goes
one season a year
then it goes
Christmas comes
again, again
presents to be opened
decorate the tree
the smell of excitement
and the joy it brings
the smell of pudding
and the roast chicken
winter and Christmas
matters to me
because of the snow
and memories it brings.

Courtney Paniczew (12)
Ryburn Valley High School, Sowerby

What Matters To Me

Running, my friends and my family
These are the things that matter to me
When I'm running a race, the wind in my hair,
I'm flying 1st place, without a single care.
When I'm bored of doing math,
It's great to be with my mates and having a laugh.
Our times together are ace but
We hang around in such a confined space
If I've had a bad day and I'm feeling glum,
I know I can come home and speak to my mum.
I love my little brother,
But he is such a bother.
Crash, crash, crashing around the place,
But he is ace.
I love my little sisters they are so much fun,
That's what matters to me, now my poem is done.

Olivia Holmes (13)
Ryburn Valley High School, Sowerby

What Matters To Me

What matters to me is dancing.
Dancing is fun, dancing is everything.
Performing in a show is exciting.
Lots of people gather to watch.
Friends and family too.
Feeling nervous now at the side of the stage.
It's my turn, fingers crossed, remember the moves.
Once I was started my fears soon departed.
I don't know why I was frightened I should have been delighted.
Because, before you know it that's it, it's over.
I want to do it all again.
Congratulations, well done, good show.
They say.
Deep breath.
Phew!

Ellese Trowell (14)
Ryburn Valley High School, Sowerby

Ice Cream

I like ice cream
Chocolate is the best
Pity it melts in a sun beam
To go without it is a hard test.

I shake sprinkles all over
And pour on tasty sauce
Then add a four leaf clover
To stop me getting brain freeze of course!

Then I sit down to eat
I raise my spoon
And tuck into the tasty treat!
I'm not going to give it up, not even to a baboon . . .

Matteo Sabelli (12)
St Bede's Catholic Grammar School, Bradford

I Wish

I've got ice in my veins,
blood in my eyes,
hate in my heart,
love in my mind,
I see nights full of pain,
hurt but never cry . . .

I wish I could just . . .
drop the world . . .

You keep the sunshine,
save me the rain,
I work but forever try,
but I'm cursed,
so never mind,
huh, my word is my pride . . .

I wish I could just . . .
drop the world . . .

I went to the bar,
ordered some wine,
no one can have it,
because it's all mine,
why did I have to be a sad, lonely widower,
couldn't I just be married to a 'Harvey Nics' modeller . . .

I wish I could just . . .
drop the world . . .

because I will
probably die . . .

Hasan Ali (11)
St Bede's Catholic Grammar School, Bradford

My Poem Is About Flowers!

I went to the tower
I took a flower
to meet my best friend
as I walked in
I fell over a bin
because I was shocked
to see who she sent
I saw this man
with a funny tan
but asked to speak to her
he called out her name
but what a shame
she was busy playing a game
I took a pen out of my coat
and wrote her a note
to say I will come again
as I walked back home
I felt so alone
but surprised to see her there
I laughed a ton
we had good fun
but then she had to go
I wanted to cry
as she said goodbye
and that's enough for tonight.

Hamza Hussain (12)
St Bede's Catholic Grammar School, Bradford

This Is Me And My Team

As I run the field I throw the ball
My teammates help me through it all,
We help each other through and through as a team
We know each other in our teens.

Josh Halpin (11)
St Bede's Catholic Grammar School, Bradford

English Lesson

I don't like English
I find it boring
When I sit down
I start snoring

If I wake up in a morning
I check my planner
I say, 'Oh no
I've got English.'

English is tough
It's too hard
I get in the class
And my brain goes to mush

I'm not allowed to move
I get in the groove
And then I get disrupted
By this weird dude

I think of the lesson
I say, 'Oh no
I'm gonna get a detention
Because I just don't know.'

Christopher Hartley (12)
St Bede's Catholic Grammar School, Bradford

Music

M usic is very passionate
U sher, Eminem and Rihanna are music legends and you could be one of them
S ound fills our body like a powerful force humming our favourite songs that we adore
I dream of becoming a recording artist
C ould I be as famous as everyone else? That's for me to know!

Amandeep Shibber (12)
St Bede's Catholic Grammar School, Bradford

What The World Means To Me

World, world you mean to me
more than my Xbox or PS3.

There's a lot of pollution killing you
people cut down but it's still true.

This is my land
which God made with His left and right hand.

You're in the middle of space
with the moon with a laughing face.

Earth and humans may not be neat
but You God gave humans, hands and feet.

There is poor and there is grand
but humans will always stand.

Even the best scientists thought you were flat
like a welcome home doormat.

Thank you for creating me
the world is wild and so free.

Adam Baldwin (13)
St Bede's Catholic Grammar School, Bradford

Mrs Gren's Hen

Mrs Gren had a hen, who was
big, fat and round and never made a sound.

It was quite white and it could be
seen very clearly at night.

One day I touched Mrs Gren's hen
on the back and it said,
'Do you want a smack?'

Then I screamed and ran away and
never saw Mrs Gren's hen again.

Isam Nafeel (11)
St Bede's Catholic Grammar School, Bradford

Grandma

Grandma, we love you
Grandma, we do
when you arrive
we just wanna hug you.

Grandma, you're great
but there's one thing we hate
and that's when our parents
come up through the gate.

We love you a lot
more than you know
and we love it when
you look after us when
it starts to snow.

Grandma we love you
that's all we can say
and can't wait to see
you the very next day.

Matthew Hines [12]
St Bede's Catholic Grammar School, Bradford

My Family

My family mean so much to me,
Our love is as strong as roots on a tree.
All my family are really caring,
We also like sharing.
We all help one and another,
Like my sister and my brother
There is also my father,
And there is also my mother.
My family mean so much to me,
Our love is as strong as roots on a tree.

Declan Craven [13]
St Bede's Catholic Grammar School, Bradford

Animals Extinct

Animals are rare
Don't strip them bare
Destroying their habitat
We'll kill them just like that

It will be a curse
So don't cut down the forest
Or it will get worse
Everyone can do something

Whatever the type
We love them
Surely someone must care
Killing creatures that live there

Keep the forest
Keep the trees
Hear the noise of the animals
Whispering through the breeze
Before we even blink it may become extinct.

Kane Scollick (11)
St Bede's Catholic Grammar School, Bradford

Everything Matters

Everything matters big or small
Everything matters even nothing at all
Everything matters life or death
All you have to do is enjoy the rest
Everything matters reality or dreams
Everything matters even life as it seems
Everything matters night or day
Everything matters everything you say
Everything matters here or there
Everything matters reader beware.

Phoenix Costello (13)
St Bede's Catholic Grammar School, Bradford

If Love Was . . .

If love was McDonald's, I'd be the Big Mac
If love was fresh breath, I'd be the Tic Tac
If love was an iPhone, I'd be the app
If love was a hiker, I'd be the map
If love was Mum, I'd be Dad
If love was anger, I'd be mad
If love was the sea, I'd be a crab
If love was an ice lolly, I'd be a Fab
If love was a bar, I'd be the beer
If love was football, I'd be the cheer
If love was a storm, I'd be the sea
If love was a door, I'd be the key
If love was a fruit, I'd be an apple
If love was God, I'd be the chapel
If love was the night, I'd be the moon
If love was music, I'd be the tune
If love was nature, I'd be a bee
If love was St Bede's, I'd be me!

Jacob Wheeler (12) & Luke Simpson (13)
St Bede's Catholic Grammar School, Bradford

Winter

The trees in our garden
have grown very tall,
the leaves are turning
red and brown and
are going to fall!

A robin hopped along our path,
I didn't show any fear,
that's a sign that summer's
gone and winter is now here!

Ollie Raistrick (11)
St Bede's Catholic Grammar School, Bradford

Moving House

We had to move house,
because of the giant mouse.
It ate through the walls,
and bust all the balls.

When we finally reached the house,
we found there was no giant mouse.
So we entered through the door,
but quickly stopped dead in awe!

What we saw was such a state,
it looked like the work of my good mate.
When it was clean,
it didn't look so mean.

We had something to eat,
and put up our feet.
Not long before banging my head,
and going to bed.

Jake Harker (12)
St Bede's Catholic Grammar School, Bradford

Games

Games, games, games so fun to play
You get your own way
Games, games, games, it's virtual, so searchable
Games, games, games, good for relaxation
Able to move around
Makes it look so realistic
Exciting to get a new one
So playable you could play all day
Games, games, games, outdoor fun
Find out who won
Games, games, games, don't forget to play fair
Or the others just won't share.

Kieran Walton (11)
St Bede's Catholic Grammar School, Bradford

I Am In Heaven With You

The day I fell for you . . .
Made me realise the pleasure of life

The way you loved me . . .
Taught me how to care in life

The pain in living apart and
The suffering of missing you

Promise to be with you always
I hope you will too . . .

Dry throat once wet,
As we finally met . . .

The reason to love you
Will always remain the same

I am in Heaven as I am with you,
I will be in Heaven as I will be with you.

Mahaz Ahmed (11)
St Bede's Catholic Grammar School, Bradford

A Poem For You Grandad

When I was three, my grandad died,
When I found out, I was petrified,
I started crying at the thought of him dying,
And I never saw him again.

He brings back memories,
And good ones too,
Making me feel better
When I am in the blue.

I miss him so much,
I wish you could see,
Just quite how much,
He means to me.

Alex Jennings (12)
St Bede's Catholic Grammar School, Bradford

Spring

While walking through the spring-like weather,
I saw a moor full of heather.

When I see the sun begin to rise,
To me it is a very good prize.

As the birds begin to twitter,
The weather is still bitter.

As the sun comes out,
All the flowers begin to sprout!

While the children merrily play,
The grass begins to sway.

As the horses trot into the meadows,
We suddenly start to realise that,
This is spring.

Matthew Adam Tordoff (11)
St Bede's Catholic Grammar School, Bradford

The Autumn Trees

The trees swayed as the wind swept
the emerald green leaves
The rain dropped onto the cold firm ground
as the leaves brushed against each other.

The white snow softly landed on to the
lifeless massive tree.
The cool crisp breeze
whipped the damp grass.
The brittle rocks swept along!
As the wind swept the streets
King, P and D walked on as the wind
ferociously hit them.

Daniel Raj (11)
St Bede's Catholic Grammar School, Bradford

School

School boring school all I hear
Do this, do that
So many boring topics
English, maths and science
I wish we did nothing
Just sit and play and play
I don't want to go to boring school
Miss shouts this is due tomorrow
I wish it would all stop.

School teachers shout, say do this, do that
All I want to do is be free from the shouting and the tests

There is only one lesson I like, PE,
Brilliant PE but only if I could do PE, rest and PE
And I would be brilliant.

Ahmad Ayub (11)
St Bede's Catholic Grammar School, Bradford

Poem About A Car

A car is a car
If it rides you nearby or far

A car is a car
When it gets you in time to the bar

A car is a car
When you are addressed as Madam/Sir

But for some
A car is just not a car
It is a home
After a bright roam
It is a home.

Jamal Madni (11)
St Bede's Catholic Grammar School, Bradford

My Family

My family is not fair.
My family do not care.
My family do not love me.
My family are not that bothered about hair.
My family all were fighting.
My family never share.
I just wonder if my family have a bit of sense.

Will my family be normal?
Will my family be friends?
Nobody knows
I wish that we were a normal family.

One day they became very generous.
My family got on.
My family are as one big happy family.

Zeeshan Khan (12)
St Bede's Catholic Grammar School, Bradford

Snowy Month

It is a dark and snowy night.
The life has faded, trees have died.
The birds have gone and taken flight.
The animals are cold, they have to hide.
My hands are red and so very sore.
Winter is leaving after all of this time.
Winter has been shown the door.
It is not hated for all of its crime.
Birds all now sing songs of joy.
On trees full of life and mixed shades of green.
Children are all sad girls and boys.
Not a spot of white to be seen.

Cameron Peacock (12)
St Bede's Catholic Grammar School, Bradford

Liverpool!

I support Liverpool
Because Liverpool's really cool,
If my cat could talk, I'm sure she would shout,
'Liverpool,' 'cause Liverpool's so cool
The spectators are not ghouls
'Cause they shout Liverpool
Liverpool is so cool and they're not made of
Liver or a pool
Yes I support Liverpool
'Cause Liverpool's so cool
If you don't like Liverpool
I am not your friend.

Aiden Doherty (11)
St Bede's Catholic Grammar School, Bradford

Surprising Season

Spring, the season of birth
the lambs are with Mother in the wide open field
and the buds on the trees ready to blossom,
the chicks in the tree.
Summer, the season of blossoming and heat,
when God sends his heart down to heat the world,
the buds blossoming into beautiful leaves.
Autumn, the season of death, the leaves die and go brown,
the animals are slaughtered for the meat,
the trees look barer like a person with no friends.
Winter, the season of cold, when God tucks up the white blanket
to keep the world warm through the cold season.

Gabriel Foster (11)
St Bede's Catholic Grammar School, Bradford

Dark And Light

In the dark of night,
In the light of day,
Take not my life away.
Dark and light, hear my might
Let the badness take flight.

Dark and light, see my fright,
Don't get caught in the dead of night.
Dark see my light,
You will not defeat my might.

James Delamarre-Spence (11)
St Bede's Catholic Grammar School, Bradford

My Rocket

My rocket was falling from the sky
The moon caught it and told it to fly
Fly away, fly away for the rest of this night
Hope that you have a good life
If anything happens come and tell me
Because your worst enemies will soon meet me.
The next day I met the sun, it said,
'Don't come any closer or I might burn you.'

Kayode Ajayi (11)
St Bede's Catholic Grammar School, Bradford

On The Beach

I was chilling on the beach
The sun in my eyes
Drinking cola to make me high
My feet on the table relaxed as could be
Listening to radio whilst eating ice cream.

Aran Kumar (11)
St Bede's Catholic Grammar School, Bradford

135

Presents

P eople give them,
R eally big and really small,
E very Christmas, Eid and birthday,
S ometimes even for nothing,
E ven money
N othing sometimes, just a hug
T oys, clothes, money
S urprise! Surprise! Surprise!

Samee Khan (11)
St Bede's Catholic Grammar School, Bradford

Tornado

The tornado a deadly creature to Earth
A never-ending killing machine
An escaped devil from Hell,
Round and round it goes destroying everything in its way,
It crashes, howls and screams,
Any more the world may end.
But will it ever end?

Jay Panter (11)
St Bede's Catholic Grammar School, Bradford

Kids

Kids are silly, kids are funny
Kids have noses that are runny.

Kids have small teeth
Kids have smelly feet.

Kids like to eat honey
Kids like to get money.

Umair Asif (11)
St Bede's Catholic Grammar School, Bradford

Fog

Creeping around town
Spreading arms majestically
Using a touch sense
Coldness on your face
With a body that's so damp
A loyal worker.

Joshua Ellis (11)
St Bede's Catholic Grammar School, Bradford

Music

M usic is a passionate
U se of sound
S tars like Eminem, Usher and BOB try fulfilling your dreams like
I wanted to. Justin Bieber, why do all the girls have a
C rush on him, it should be me!

Cameron Hill (12)
St Bede's Catholic Grammar School, Bradford

Mysterious Me!

I'm a puzzle, I'm full of clues
I'm a ball of fire
But you treat me like a scratty old tyre
You try to discover the secrets I hide
You'll be swished away like a helpless shell on the tide.

Hasnain Khalid (12)
St Bede's Catholic Grammar School, Bradford

Lost!

As I step away from the path I feel as if I am heading for a new world.
I walk gently through the mystic forest, thinking about every step I make.
The winds blow coldly against my pale face
A cold chill races quickly down my neck . . .
I hear the trees rustling, rustling as if it is a warning for me not to go on . . .

Dreadful thoughts fill my head
More and more thoughts take over my mind
Every second is fear,
The fear which eats me up alive . . .

A thought comes on me like a wave invading a rock
Should I go on,
On to this unexplored, unknown world
Or should I go back and never know what lies ahead of me?

Sofia Terreros Martin (13)
St Bede's School, Scunthorpe

My Ballet Shoes Have Grown Skin Deep

My ballet shoes have grown skin deep
I'll twist and twirl
I can dance all night
From dawn to dusk
From dark to light
You can't stop me it's in my feet
My ballet shoes have grown skin deep.

My ballet shoes have grown skin deep
I'll dance in school just in my mind
I'll miss whole subjects
One at a time
I zone out not listen like most kids do
But I am still wearing my ballet shoes
You can't stop me it's in my feet
My ballet shoes have grown skin deep.

Poppy Louise Dale (11)
Sheffield High School, Sheffield

Deforestation

I am the last one.
I am the lone survivor.

Before me, a battlefield of strewn bodies,
The corpses of my brothers,
Wounded irreversibly,
Burnt and decayed,
Slaughtered for their skin,
One by one, slashed and murdered,
My family gone,
Only stumps left as shadows,
Leaving me naked,
Exposed in all my anguish.

The Grim Reaper strolls forward,
The infamous scythe absent,
Replaced with a glinting axe,
His path littered with crumpled leaves,
Wrinkled before their time,
His path leads to me.
I am next.

Greed-corrupted spirits march closer,
Led by the Reaper's flag of death,
I am on the front line,
The last brave soldier.
Their cleavers will rip,
Hack into my hide,
And as I scream,
So will Mother Nature.

I am the last one.
I am the lone survivor.

Shalaka Darshane (17)
Sheffield High School, Sheffield

My Angel

I need your wings fluttering outside,
Keeping watch through the keyhole,
And in the world's darkening light,
Living in vain are all the people.

But in the summer, on a dying day,
My friend you had to fly away,
And the snow of despair is all I could see,
'I'll be back,' is the last thing you said to me.

Fly away, my spirit to the red daybreak,
To the black day.
The sun - a white sphere,
Sheltered me from those dark wings.
Hey, how could you do this to me?
My angel.

Oh angel,
Standing upon my right shoulder,
Acting like you're not there,
Keeping your mouth tightly shut.
While I search for you elsewhere.
If I cry out to you one more time,
Will you appear in front of me?
Again I'm lost, I'm paralysed,
By the beckoning stars so I pray
That my guardian angel might say,
'I'm back.'

Fly away, my spirit to the red daybreak,
To the black day.
The sun - a white sphere,
Sheltered me from those dark wings.
Hey, how could you do this to me?
My angel.

Angelic protector, my satellite
You who couldn't see,
You who flew away,
The stars followed you and left me
Somewhere, there was a sign I did see

Yet you,
I lost.

Fly away, my spirit to the red daybreak,
To the black day.
The sun - a white sphere,
Sheltered me from those dark wings.
Hey, how could you do this to me?
My angel

Fly away, my spirit, my soul . . .
My angel.

Zahera Khan [14]
Sheffield High School, Sheffield

Woof!

Early in the morning,
Without any warning,
Woof!
Tails are wagging,
Excited and panting,
Woof!
Waiting for feeding,
And then walking,
Woof!
Walking and running,
And lots of pulling,
Woof!
Sniff, sniff, sniffing,
Playing and fetching,
Woof!
Always licking,
Stroking and cuddling,
Woof!
And that's why they matter to me,
Dogs!

Hannah Bolderson [12]
Sheffield High School, Sheffield

What Matters To You?

Family matters to me
They are always there.
No matter how far,
They will always care.

The pets that keep me warm,
On a freezing winter's day,
The sun that helps me see,
And the feel of the hot beaming ray.

The wonderful sounds of music,
Always fills my ears,
Someone plays the sweet violin,
It makes you cry tears.

Friends are fantastic,
They are the best,
That's what friends are for,
But they can be a pest!

I love the way the stars,
Come out at night,
The Chinese fairy tale,
About the moon shining bright.

The charming Earth,
Magical forests and waterfalls,
That sky at night deep in space,
Nature always calls.

The most important in life,
This is all true,
What do you think?
What matters to you?

Victoria Brown (11)
Sheffield High School, Sheffield

Peace

So tell me now, what is peace?
Is it a time when everything seems to decease?
Is it a time when all our woes and foes,
Just disappear behind their dusty doors,
Or all together escape and decrease?
Or is it a time when new life is made,
When events are forgotten of things done and said,
When together we sit by the heated hearth,
Or when we gaze at the stars, and tell stories of the Earth,
Or when we dust down our bikes and ride in the spring,
When we leap for joy, shout and sing,
Or when we lie in our beds snugly and warm,
And consider our lives as a blessing?
So before you open your mouth to criticise,
The life you live and the people you love,
Consider those who are more in need,
Those who have suffered from other's greed,
We should live life in the moments and support a good cause,
To love and to cherish, to wait and to pause,
Stop,
Think,
Don't live life too fast,
Choose the right paths for your happiness to last,
Stand for what you believe in, and fight for what's right,
Don't stand by and watch others fall from great height,
Pray for deliverance and educate the wrong,
Teach them God's way through praise and through song,
So then one day when everything seems to cease,
When we are quiet within our hearts, content and at ease,
Then will we know the true meaning of peace.

Lyn Muzulu (15)
Sheffield High School, Sheffield

Xara

January 1999 born to David and Jane,
Whose life from then would never be the same,

And though born in Sheffield I didn't live there,
I lived in Northampton though my memories are rare,

I ventured to Sheffield aged about 4, I think,
To a lovely big house and a bedroom of pink,

When I started at school I attended Ashdell,
I tried to work hard and hoped I'd do well.

Travelling allowed me to go near and far,
Over sea, air and land, by ship, plane and car,

I've flown to Dubai, taken a Disneyland cruise,
And visited Calais, to get my dad's booze.

To travelling with Mum whose job is to fly,

And of course Center Parcs and good old Cornwall,
I love there for surfing, the best waves of all.

My auntie says I was born with webbed feet,
In swimming I race hard with opposition to beat,

The Sheffield City is my local team,
And a gold winning medal is my aim and dream,

Now I'm eleven, independent and glad,
I'm as tall as my mum with more hair than my dad.

I'll continue to work hard in both work and play,
And my future . . .

. . . well that's a poem for another day.

Xara Harrison (11)
Sheffield High School, Sheffield

My Family And Other Animals

My family is rather small,
In fact it's hardly there at all,
My mum, my dad, my brother (brat!)
We also have about six cats.

I say about six cats you see,
As point of fact twixt you and me,
They move so fast it's hard to tell,
There could be five, or six as well.

Our house was once quite new and smart,
Its walls adorned with drapes and art,
But having cats who love to play,
Has turned our once white walls to grey,

Our sofas once so full of fluff,
Are leaking out all of their stuff,
The curtains hang from shiny rails,
Perfect for cats to sharpen nails.

The rugs we have upon the floor,
Are where our cats lie down and snore,
For creatures only weighing pounds,
They make some truly awful sounds.

And that is why in our four walls,
No passer-by or friend e'er calls,
The cats have scared them off you see,
In fact they also frighten me!

Maybe we should get a dog?

Olivia Casapieri (11)
Sheffield High School, Sheffield

Mine

His soft padded hands latch into bony knees
And his grooved back slots into the deep purple scratches
Of the wall, vein-like in the flickering light.

The muffled drilling, pounding rhythmically,
Lulling him gently into silence.
His head, cocked,
Eyes fixed on the tunnel,
Lips parted - waiting.

Waiting for its suffocating darkness
To be slashed by a wrapped parcel of food
Tumbling
    Violently
        Down.

The cold air hits him, wakes him, makes him rise.
Jolted forward he is thrust and pulled at by
Unfriendly metal tongs.
Ripped out into thunderous noise he is born.

Fierce sunlight slams against his body.
Stiff limbs and a pallid face are groped
As he is inspected by a thousand cameras' blinking eyes.
He flexes and stumbles, walking slowly
And with trepidation.

He meets his mother's gaze, at last,
And she runs to him, to hold him.

Her baby.

Jessica Denniff (15)
Sheffield High School, Sheffield

What Matters To Me?

Happiness matters to me . . .
Happiness is so very dear,
It can go like that and never reappear,
Happiness brightens every day,
Even in the smallest of ways.

Dreams matter to me . . .
Dreams make you who you are,
Although some go a bit too far,
It's all about who you are,
And who you want to be,
Fairy tales or life itself, it's all the same to me.

Memories matter to me . . .
Good or bad they can be,
But whatever kind, it's still worth its keep,
You remember for a reason,
No matter how strange they can be,
New births, married life, or just a chatty friendly meet,
Some important, some less so,
All memories!

Love matters to me . . .
Love outshines problems,
Whatever they can be,
It lifts you up when you are down,
And can spin you all around,
Up and down it goes,
But always returns when it matters the most!

Charlotte Elizabeth Wilson (11)
Sheffield High School, Sheffield

Twinkle

I love my little teddy, Twinkle
He's a part of life for me
If I lost him, I don't know what I'd do
He's a special thing, you see!

His neck, it's worn, well, yes I know,
It's as thin as can be!
But I love my little Twinkle
And I think that he loves me!

To hide poor Twinkle's weight loss
He wears a jumper that is red
It has white edges, with a big white heart,
And a hole for Twinkle's head!

Every night he sleeps with me,
Tucked up in my bed
He sits there all night silent
And listens to what's been said!

Old Twinks, he has a great big heart
For such a little bear,
And my love for him is always there
Even though he is threadbare

I love my little teddy, Twinkle
He's a part of life for me
If I lost him, I don't know what I'd do
He's a special thing, you see!

Lucy Bower (11)
Sheffield High School, Sheffield

What Matters To Me

Sport

What matters to me?

Sport matters to me when the tension builds up in my legs before I run and leap, when everyone cheers for me when I jump far!
The happiness when I get into the finals!
When I get to the post in netball and take a shot and I score!

Family

What matters to me?

My family matters to me when my mum takes me shopping and when my dad comes on the trampoline with us and I go *mega* high!
And when my sister asks me to play dollies with her, when I play Star Wars with my brother!

Friends

What matters to me?

My friends matter to me when me and my gang used to mess around at my old school and see each other at the weekend!

Pets

What matters to me?

My pets matter to me when my dog Honey howls at musical instruments and my chickens have chicks!

Holly Smith (11)
Sheffield High School, Sheffield

Sun

I like the sun
it matters to me
without the sun
where would I be?
Without the sun
I would be sad
without the sun
life would be bad
without the sun
no birds would sing
that would be a dreadful thing
aliens from far and
aliens from wide
use the sun as a navigation guide
creatures from high and
creatures down low
without a sun
have nowhere to go
when the sun comes out I dance with glee
it makes me feel warm and happy
I like the sun
that's why it matters to me.

Elizabeth Bartolomé (11)
Sheffield High School, Sheffield

What Matters To Me

Pick up a book, what do you see?
A whole new world opens for me
Heroes and villains dance over the pages
Fighting each other across the ages.

Reading a book, what do you hear?
Swordfights crash across the ear
Fairies flutter peacefully by
Their wingbeats become a gentle sigh.

Pick up a book, what do you feel?
The daring pirates seem so real
The nightmare creeps slowly on
You can't breathe a breath until it's gone.

Reading a book, what can you smell?
Medieval feasts and desserts as well
Through a meadow the aroma of flowers
The sweet fresh scent of April showers.

Reading a book, what shall it be?
Garth Nix or Cathy Cassidy
Dragons and knights or modern day
What will you find along the way?

Nadia Rickards (11)
Sheffield High School, Sheffield

My Pillow

The fluffy feathers in it,
Give it a loving feel,
And I keep it beside me,
To make my mistakes heal.

It helps me like a fairy,
It never gets too cross,
And when I rest my head on it,
It makes it want to toss.

I keep it in my warm bed,
It tells me right and wrong,
If I get too weak alone,
It comes and makes me strong.

Whenever something happens,
I rush into my bed,
And tell it my queries then,
I act out what it said.

I'll always love my cushion,
And keep it nice and well,
And then I will stay beside it,
With more stories to tell.

Ankita Sharma (11)
Sheffield High School, Sheffield

Horses

H orses with expensive bloodlines
O rdinary scruffy ponies but as special,
R unning wild and free forever,
S trong creatures with flowing manes, in
E very way they're amazing!
S uperhuman racing machines . . .

Rebbecca Newton (12)
Sheffield High School, Sheffield

What Matters To Me?

My family are very special to me
They love and care and cook my tea
There's Grandma, Grandad, my sister, Abbie
Aunts and uncles, Mummy and Daddy!

I got my teddy, Tommie, when I was three
He sleeps in bed each night with me
Even though his fur is going
My love for him carries on growing

Playing music is lots of fun
I play clarinet duets with my mum
I'm in the concert band at school
Being musical is really cool

I've been at high school a short while now
It's wonderful and I will tell you how
It's hard work but rewarding and good fun too
I've made lots of friends, it's brill
Thank you.

Rebekah Pepper (11)
Sheffield High School, Sheffield

Pain

Pain.
The icy river that burns
As it wraps its cold tendrils
Around your heart
Sometimes you think you've managed
To get through it,
Out of the river.
Not for long.
Once you're in its torturous embrace,
There is no escape.
It grips me now.

Ella Shaw (16)
Sheffield High School, Sheffield

Formula One

Michael Schumacher is a cheat,
Jimmy Clark's driving was quite neat,
Eddie Jordan made his own team up,
Barrichello has never won the cup.

Abu Dhabi is very flash,
Spa always gives us a crash,
Singapore is done at night,
Monza's corners are always tight.

McLaren make marvellous machines,
Ferrari favour Fernando, who's mean,
Stewart racing had to pull out,
Cos their finances were in doubt.

The BBC mean a lot to me,
When they show this on the TV,
All the people that make it what it is,
Let the victory champagne go *fizz, fizz, fizz!*

Lucinda Armstrong (11)
Sheffield High School, Sheffield

Important Things

Important things in my life are free
This means my family
The first thing is my mum who looks after me
My nana and grandad
Are all so kind
They really love and care for me
I have aunties and uncles
Whom I love and adore
My fish and my dog
Who I sometimes take for a jog
It's very important to have a family
We all live very happily.

Heidi Rowland (11)
Sheffield High School, Sheffield

A Collection Of Matter

An island protecting me from the rest of the world -
My home.
Freedom to express myself -
Music.
Someone I can trust -
Solid friendship.
Saving the one and only -
Planet Earth.
They're always there -
My family.
Something to laugh at and to play with -
My pets.
Recalling the past -
Memories.
Looking at things that have gone -
Photos.
What matters to you?

Olivia Jowle (11)
Sheffield High School, Sheffield

Annabelle Claire

My Christian names are Annabelle Claire
And I do always try to be fair
I have recently started at Sheffield High
And my dream is to aim for the sky.
To be a lawyer is what I will be
Depending on grades, of course, we shall see!
At the moment I'm quite happy to play
Hockey, netball and tennis I say,
My family are great you can see!
Especially Ted who sits on my knee.
The only problem is my elder brother
But even he I wouldn't swap for another!

Annabelle Burgin (11)
Sheffield High School, Sheffield

Hockey

. . . The score two all with two minutes to go.
I was scared running with the ball, going for goal
as my coach was screaming from the sideline . . .

I'm talking about hockey
My game and my name
My love and my life

I'm thinking about hockey
My game and my name
The place I feel at home

I'm dreaming about hockey
My game and my name
Like a holiday at home

I'm dreaming, thinking, talking and loving
hockey and then I shoot
Goal!

Natasha Jones (11)
Sheffield High School, Sheffield

What Matters To Me

Happiness matters to me,
Having fun with friends and family,
Seeing smiley, happy faces,
Taking thrills at very fast paces!

Sadness matters to me,
The fun is gone too quickly,
Sulking around, feeling sorry for yourself,
At least you're in good health!

Feelings matter very much to me;
Between these two I'd much rather be . . .
Happy!

Megan Newell-Price (11)
Sheffield High School, Sheffield

What Matters To You?

There are lots of things that matter to me,

I like to shop,
My brother likes to swim,
My mum likes bags,
And my dad, well this is him,
He loves fast cars,
He loves big boats,

But all these things they can't really be that important,
What is?
Could it be my pets?
Could it be my friends?
Could it be winning
Or putting the lids on my pens?

Whether it's sport, shopping, fast cars or pets,
The one thing that matters to me is being the best!

Kate Field (11)
Sheffield High School, Sheffield

Tomorrow

A world without any animals,
Would be no world at all.

A world with war and hatred would be a world of savages,
No safe place to stay, no street fit to walk.

A world without flowers, no shrubbery, no trees,
What would this world be like, with no colour to see?

A world of pollution and litter would be a harmful world,
Not right for life, not right for you or me.

A world without people would have no life,
Would not breathe air, would not make sounds.

What if this was your tomorrow?

Hannah Grunwerg (11)
Sheffield High School, Sheffield

What Can You See?

I can see the pixies flying in the flowers,
I can see the wind curl up the Eiffel Tower,
I can see the clouds floating in the sky,
I can see the circus of birds flying high,
I can see a shooting star at night,
I can see the theatre and the spotlight,
I can see the water dazzling as it should,
I can see the people cutting trees for wood,
I can see the angels talking to one and another,
I can see the children laughing with each other,
I can see the music as wild as can be,
I can see the sun hanging above the sea,
I can see the books whisper about themselves,
I can see a pot of gold and tiny little elves,
I can see the animals showing their affection,
I can see a mirror and my wonderful reflection.

Isha Mordekar [11]
Sheffield High School, Sheffield

What Matters To Me?

Cuddling my soft, fluffy hamster's fur,
Staying up all night worrying about him sleeping in the sink.
Being in my bedroom listening to music or on the computer.
Feeding my kitten, Oliver, some juicy chicken legs.
Practising my singing in the house.
Watching my hamster, Nibbles, roll about in his ball.
Walking round in all of my shoes and dresses.
Playing with my adorable kitten, Oliver, all day.
Drawing pictures in my spare time.
Being with my family all day long.
Making cards for special occasions.
Cuddling my favourite toy cat every single day.
Playing with all of my friends on school days.

Charlotte Anne Hogg [12]
Sheffield High School, Sheffield

What Matters To Me!

Memories are life experiences,
Memories stay close to me, never far, they're right beside us.

Sadness and happiness are part of our memories.
Losing something makes it a memory like breaking your mum's
favourite vase.

Memories are kept in our minds like a box, some memories are sweet,
some are sour.

I sparkle inside when I remember happy, funny thoughts, I feel damp when I
remember upsetting thoughts.

Every step we take is part of our memories;
I sneakily have a peek at the memories at night.

Memories are beautiful events.
I can't wait for the next adventure.

Hannah Rose Aziz (11)
Sheffield High School, Sheffield

The Great British 4

Rain, thunder, fog, sun, snow, hail.
Some of the great British weather;
Spring, summer, autumn, winter we all moan about it
saying it's annoying, unpredictable, dreary, boring and so on.
Do we look at the positives?
Sometimes we do have the spells of luck
occasionally the sun equals
ice cream, suncream and visits to the beach
but the rain equals
raincoats, umbrellas and indoor breaks.
But why don't we give this weather a break?
Why don't we embrace it and don't let it get us down?
So go out and cherish it.

Farzana Yasmin (11)
Sheffield High School, Sheffield

Home

The place where everything is,
Family and our possessions,
The good times we have spent with each other, there,
Christmases spent by the fire eating succulent mince pies,
And sharing the happy Christmas cheer with loved ones,
Children's first words and steps were there.

The warm cocoon, keeping everyone within safe and happy,
With a room for everyone stuffed with soft cuddly toys,
And lots of furniture.

It started as an empty, lifeless building, meaning nothing to anyone,
Empty rooms, empty corridors and no characteristics at all!
However the day we moved into that empty lifeless building,
It became warm and full of life,
Home, *our home.*

Helen Singleton (11)
Sheffield High School, Sheffield

All About Me

Beautiful music,
Gorgeous sound,
Playing all day,
Makes music go round!

Sizzling cooking,
Chopping sounds,
Preparing food,
Swallowing it down!

Amazing sport,
Ducking and diving,
All of the day,
Can't wait till the next day to play!

Casey Oades (11)
Sheffield High School, Sheffield

What Matters To Me?

The day that I went to the beach,
Was the best day of my life,

The soft gentle sand that swayed through my feet
The cold but beautiful sea that lay there like a sheet.

The mouth-watering doughnuts that tasted like Heaven,
The huge sandcastles that would stand as still as Devon,

The day went by as fast as ever,
But it's never going to be gone forever,

The memories are behind and the future is to come,
But until then your memories will be great fun!

Maria Hussain (11)
Sheffield High School, Sheffield

What Matters To Me

What matters to me
Is who I am.

What matters to me
Is how I'll be.

What matters to me
Is what I'll see.

What matters to me
Is friends and family.

What matters to me
Is everything going pleasantly.

Charlotte Grace Waddington (12)
Sheffield High School, Sheffield

My Teddy

I have one thing that matters to me,
A little purple teddy full of glee.

With a perfect smile you should see,
And the great big hug he gives to me.
Cotton coming off his nose,
With little battered feet and toes.
As the years have gone by he's begun to fade,
But I think he's as good as when he was first made.

This teddy of mine is *my* very best friend,
And *our* special friendship will never end.

Katie Bricklebank (11)
Sheffield High School, Sheffield

Alfie, My Cat

A lways full of energy
L ively, cute and curious
F luffy, white and soft to touch
I love him very much
E very night exploring

M ovements in the dark
Y earning for a mouse to come

C atch it if he can
A nxious and waiting for the pounce
T ime is running out.

Chloe Penty (12)
Sheffield High School, Sheffield

What Matters To Me

The sloppy lipstick kisses from my grandma on a crispy
winter's dawn,
And the heart warming thought of a baby being born,
The feeling of my puppy's ruby fur on my face,
And the thrill of a walk in the countryside every second,
every pace.

The tear of a God landing on my nose,
And fine sand slipping through my toes,
Can you imagine what I see
In all the things that matter to me?

Elizabeth Capps (11)
Sheffield High School, Sheffield

Things That Matter To Me

M e on my own in my room.
Y awning, stretching in the early morning.

B eing myself and chilling out.
E ating my tea whilst watching TV.
D oing my homework with my mum's help.
R eading, writing, concentrating hard.
O pening my covers and slipping in.
O pening my eyes to the light streaming in.
M y bedroom means a lot to me because my bedroom's mine.

Caris Songhurst (11)
Sheffield High School, Sheffield

What Matters To Me

D arting across the floor
A pplying yourself to do the best
N ew skills learned every day
C oupéing the bar
I ndecisive of the next move
N ot sure what is going to happen
G alloping gracefully around the room.

Katie Bower (11)
Sheffield High School, Sheffield

Memories

Every memory is locked in our minds,
and some things never leave us.
Arms reach out through time and space,
to hold those special memories in place.
Memories are bad things and sad things.
Everyone has them, unique to us all.

Remember them wisely,
In life they might help.

Libby Bloodworth (11)
Sheffield High School, Sheffield

Freedom

F ighting for freedom in this lonely, dense world.
R ights are always heard, why aren't children's rights heard?
E nding slavery is the only option.
E ating disorder is the way our life runs.
D ancing and sports is not in our dictionary.
O rdering us 24/7, is that the only hobby?
M any centuries will pass, but one day we will all be free.

Rajvir Kaur Puni (11)
Sheffield High School, Sheffield

Shadow Of The Night

Silent, sharp
Shadows
Slipping through
The cold, clear night
Sly, skilful masters
Of deception
Stalking their prey
Like foxes on a
Midnight hunt

Ever searching
Ever seeking
New territories
And prey
Swift as a
Night flight
Hawk
Stalking unwary
Prey

The shadows
Of the night
Are watchful
Ever so
Staring at
Its pitiful
Prey like
A panther
Upon its
Unworthy foe

The shadows
Engulf the night

Till the break
Of dawn
Then the shadows
Sleep, sleep,
Sleep
But when the
Shadowed night
Falls
No one will
Be safe.

Robert Petrie (13)
Sir John Nelthorpe School, Brigg

Where My Heart Lies

The world lies before me,
Life everywhere,
The sun bounces off everything,
The trees sway with the wind,
A river leads the way to my destiny,
A bridge is over it.
Do I cross or do I follow the river to where my heart lies?
I can follow the flock, the river,
Or I can chose my own way,
I have to choose my own way, I don't want to
Follow other decisions, or their mistakes,
My opinion is just as valid as theirs,
So I cross the bridge.

Samantha Bayliss (13)
Skegness Academy, Skegness

Happy Halloween

Children dressing up
Mum's having a coffee in their special cup,
Prepare to scream on this holiday
Watch out while the ghost floats away.

Happy Halloween is here at last
Meet that zombie from the past,
Chocolate toffee everywhere
Enter the horror house if you dare.

Children run around
Nowhere to be found,
Shouting it's all you hear
Terrifying sounds is all you hear.

Happy Halloween here we come
Adults stand still and go numb,
They stay out till midnight
As they frighten people with a spooky light.

Children scream and shout
Some go for a walk about,
Vampires sucking blood
Witches using magic to create a flood.

Happy Halloween has gone and done
Children back as school are stuck in a slum,
I hope you enjoy all the fun
Look forward to the next one.

Happy Halloween.

Jasmine Shuard (11)
Skegness Academy, Skegness

Hamsterfish!

Graham was a rally driver,
He drove his car pretty quick.
He bet his best mate, Mark, a fiver,
That his driving could make Mark sick.

So they went ahead the deal,
Graham span his car around.
Mark clapped his hands like a seal
But his sick wouldn't hit the ground.

Graham began to shiver,
He thought he might lose his crash
So he drove his car into a river
With an almighty splash.

The car began to float
All the way downstream
As if it was a real boat
Mark began to scream.

'You know I get car sick, you know that's a fact
I don't like being aboard
In case we're attacked, in case we're attacked
You can't make me feel assured!'

And all that vigorous bobbing
Just bouncing up and down
Mark suddenly starting sobbing
And his smile turned into a frown.

Graham knew that he'd won
The best bet of his life
So to Mark's head he lined a gun
But Mark he had a knife.

As Graham prepared the fatal shot
Mark said, 'I'm not being funny,'
In a rage Graham said, 'What?
Kill me and there's no money!'

So they both put their weapons down,
On the count of three.
The inside of their pants turned brown

When they noticed they'd reached the sea!
I'm not trying to make this sound,
Like a scene from Jaws,
But they were frightened when they found
Some razor-sharp Hamsterfish claws!

Joe Marshall [13]
Skegness Academy, Skegness

Non-Believer

I don't believe in werewolves
Or witches, or zombies, or ghosts,
I don't believe in haunted houses,
Surrounded by big blue moats.

Dragons, sea serpents and wizards,
It's obvious they are not real,
Some people get really scared of them,
But that's not how I feel!

It wasn't 'til that day,
I heard a knock at my door,
A vampire cackling loudly,
Cackling for more and more!

I assumed it wanted my blood,
So I ran and dived on Mum's feet,
I closed my eyes and heard them say:
'Trick or treat?'

I stood up with a red face,
It was some of my friends from school,
They laughed, joked and pointed at me,
And I felt like a complete fool.

I believe in all sorts of creatures,
Ever since that horrible day,
And how do I know what's out there,
What the world has to display . . .

Chloe Blades [11]
Skegness Academy, Skegness

What Love Leads Too...

I stand at the window,
I've barricaded the door;
Trapped.
Now they can't get in.
I hear the wail.
See the flashing blue lights.
But what to do?

I can't be without,
But without I am.
Too late now,
Wish it wasn't.
Dead;
He's dead!
And the blood, it won't wash.
It's stained my hands,
And as I cry I see his face.
Remember his smile,
And regret, oh I feel regret!
But the pain still remains,
And the venom that came from his mouth, that poisoned his words.

I remember those words,
Love he told me,
Love he swore!
He swore to love me,
And the girl, the one who did this, so innocent and young
How can it be?
He loved me!
I know he did, but she poisoned his mind, changed his ways.
He loves her, he told me so.

I took the knife and plunged it deep.
Pain on his face.
Blood on my hands, and oh the blood, it flowed and flowed,
Until he had no more.
And now I stand, the bloody knife in my hand, and pull back,
If only; if only he loved me.
Then I sigh, plunge the knife and throw forward.
Then darkness.

Summer Atlanta Redford (13)
Skegness Academy, Skegness

The Sun Has Set

The sun has set in a velvet sky,
Stars twinkle and blink.
Three shadows upon a hedgerow
Poachers abroad, poachers abroad.

Down the valley and up the hill,
There's empty sacks,
They hope to fill with a well fed bunny,
And perhaps a hare.
Keepers beware, keepers beware.

A hoot of an owl the fluttering shape of a bat.
The lowing of cattle.
The bleating of sheep.
Sleep little children, sleep
Sleep little children, sleep.

Screams echo throughout the night.
Gives, a roosting cock, pheasants quite a fright.
Good people sleep sound in your beds tonight
Do not fear, do not fear.

The sky is now tinged with the rising sun,
A sleepy old keeper goes out with his gun,
But he does not see many rabbits run.
Poachers have gone, poachers have gone.

Lucy Turner (14)
Skegness Academy, Skegness

School Time

Arriving at the gates
Always late
This is what happens
Assembly at Wembley
Dram-a-rama
The wrath of maths
Manic music
Science appliance
Inkish English
Break time for fun
Then we start art
Cranky RE
Boggy history
Dreary geography
Then there's lunch
PE is good for me
Cooking puts me in the
Mood for food
Then you stood to make
Wood
French you sit on
The bench
But home time is
The best that's
When you get to
Rest.

Zak Howseman (12)
Skegness Academy, Skegness

War And Remembrance

Bent over like prisoners being beaten,
Trembling knees, coughing like hags, we trudged through the sludge.
Still seeing haunting flares, we turned our backs.
Men marching asleep. Many had lost their boots,
But we stumbled on blood-shed.
Drunk with tiredness we carried on.

Bombs, bombs quick men
Fitting the clumsy helmets just in time,
But someone was yelling and asking for help,
Dim, through the misty panes, I saw him drowning.
He plunges at me, guttering, choking, drowning.

Behind the wagon we flung him in, see his eyes
Writhing in his face, his floppy face, like a Devil sick of sin,
If you were here, at every jolt you would see
The blood come out of his mouth.

You would not tell with such zest the old lie:
Dulce et decorum est pro patria mori.

Amy Louise Woodward [12]
Skegness Academy, Skegness

Home

Home is a place of your own
Sometimes high and sometimes low
Where friends and family gather together
Where love and care are found
Your home is your home
It's what you make it.

Charlotte Rymell [12]
Skegness Academy, Skegness

Home

Cold, wet and windy outside,
I sat in my room as the summer died,
With the fire blowing,
And outside it was snowing,
This is what I call home.

Love, warmth and cosy inside,
The living room is where all my hopes start to fly,
With the TV blurring,
And my cat purring,
This is what I call home.

Smells, tastes and sights still to see,
My home always revolves around me,
I love this house,
More than a rat or a mouse,
And this is what I call home.

Emma Angrave (12)
Skegness Academy, Skegness

My Life With Diabetes

Life changed for me,
When I was three,
Things would never be the same,
Daily blood tests,
What a pain,
Insulin injections four times a day,
Carb counting is part of my life,
So confusing in my brain,
Oh no! Not again,
Diabetes is here to stay,
I deal with it every day,
Visit the clinic every three months,
It's a condition that I manage,
It's not contagious,
It's *me*, my life.

Ryan Poyser (12)
Skegness Academy, Skegness

Home

Home is a snug and cosy bed.
Home is smelling hot stew and dumplings bubbling in the oven.
Home is a place to spend Christmas with your family to celebrate the festive season.
Home is where you bake scrumptious delicious cakes.
Home is where you drink hot chocolate after building snowmen in the cold snow so deep.
Home is a warm beautiful place.
Home is where you feel most safe.
Home is where love surrounds you and your family.
Home is where you smell jam tarts being baked as you walk through the door.
Home is where the heart is.

Isaac Turner (12)
Skegness Academy, Skegness

Do You Feel Like I Do?

Cold, frosty snow crunching under my feet,
The freezing winter winds mingled in with sleet,
I felt a warm hand clad in a glove,
Hold tight onto my own hand, and yet, why don't I feel loved?

The owner of that hand slowly spoke to me,
He told me I'd be fine, he told me not to leave.
Oh, but why do I believe those lies? I can tell he doesn't care!
Yet, I know I'll open up to him. My life, with him, I'll share.

People say that love is undying when true,
And I know that words cannot express my feelings for you.
If what we share is pure enough, if you feel like I do,
Then I'll know we can't be stopped - I'll know I'll love you.

Trevyn Bell (13)
Skegness Academy, Skegness

Tommy

Scurrying around the ground,
Like a bullet making no sound,
Tommy, my little grey rodent,
With him I enjoy every moment,
Tommy's the best,
Better than all the rest,
He is the cutest thing I've ever seen,
When he is in his wheel he is really keen,
Sometimes he can be a pest,
Because he makes noises at night but he is still the best,
He's my treasure each and every day!

Katy Dixon (11)
Skegness Academy, Skegness

Home

Home is the echo of laughter
Home is dreams ever after
Home is the feeling of a goodnight kiss
Home is full of sun not fog or mist
Home is not mean
Home is like a dream
Home is for you and me
Home is where we want to be.

Casey Scott (11)
Skegness Academy, Skegness

Sisters

Sisters can be annoying but also fun,
Every time together is a special one.
Treasure every moment as they won't come again,
Loving and caring they are all the same.
You've got to love them even if they're insane,
And sometimes when they are totally lame.
Happy or sad they'll always be there,
So knowing all this, treat them with care.

Stephanie Lowis (14)
Skegness Academy, Skegness

Beast In The Woods

She ran as fast as she could
Running from the beast
In the deep dark wood.

Her terror blinded her
There was nothing she could do
She didn't make it to the present
Just like me or you.

Lydia Smith (13)
Skegness Academy, Skegness

True Friends

A true friend will be there to catch you if you fall
True friends won't give you a choice between them and others
True friends will stand up for you in a fight
True friends fight but they will always get through it.
True friends are like me and you.

Luren Ashleigh Hall (13)
Skegness Academy, Skegness

Unique

There's nothing wrong with standing out
Be yourself and no one else
No matter how you look
Or how you dress
As long as people accept your best.

Emma Burgin (13)
Skegness Academy, Skegness

What Matters To Me . . . 360

What matters to me?
Yeah I'll tell thee
It's my Xbox
360

I'd play it all day
I'd play it all night
If I could
I really would alright

Halo's my favourite
COD coming up after that
My favourite superhero game
Yep, it's the bat

The Xbox is nothing without Xbox live
Chatting with my friends online
And beating them on Halo
All the time

So the Xbox means a lot to me
Well, there is my family
But where would I be
Without my Xbox 360?

Liam Ryde (11)
Temple Moor High School, Leeds

Sport

If you do not play sport
I will build a giant fort
Football, rugby, tennis, whatever
Just play a sport forever and ever.

Daniel Jagger (12)
Temple Moor High School, Leeds

Football

A kick of a ball,
Into the hall,
It hits someone tall,
And made him fall,

One goal I scored,
It came up on the board,
The other team looked torn,
A new star was born,

When I play important matches,
I will never forget scoring hattricks,
I hope I never have one of these off form patches,
I wish the England manager was watching.

The ref blows his whistle,
That means it's time for our dismissal,
To leave I need the manager's permission,
Thinking about next week's mission.

Joseph Macklam (13)
Temple Moor High School, Leeds

Funny Me

Hey this is me,
I hate RE,

I love to draw,
I love to paint, but I
Always faint,

I am a technology king,
Well that's what I think,
And I like to drink,
I love creating things and
I fly in my dreams.

Tomasz Krupa (11)
Temple Moor High School, Leeds

Books

I love books and books love me.
Facts, folk and fantasy,
Enchanted woods and magical trees,
I love books and books love me.

I love books and books love me.
Science novels, mysteries,
Stars and planet histories.
I love books and books love me.

I love books and books love me,
Girls, kids, boys and teens.
All the things that make you scream.
I love books and books love me.

I love books and books love me.
Fact or fiction, clues or keys,
All are great just read and see!
I love books and books love me.

Alex Walker [12]
Temple Moor High School, Leeds

The Storm!

Torrential rain smashing against the grotty gravel,
Thunder claps and bangs in the air.
Lightning strikes in the stormy sky like daggers,
Dark angry clouds gathering like an army ready to fight.
A blanket of mist smothers the air.
Deafening thunder screams louder and louder.
Rain devouring anything in its path.
Gulls shrieking as the rain falls.
Lightning crackles like popping popcorn.
It's all horrendous.

Georgia Gibson [11]
Temple Moor High School, Leeds

My Daddy

Oh, how I do,
Love my dad,
He is silly and funny,
And never gets mad.

You taught me how to walk,
You taught me how to talk,
My first word was 'dada',
I turn to you and say 'cana' . . .

Things are fun when you are around,
No better Dad could ever be found,
You're the greatest kind of Daddy,
Any kind of kid could ever havvi.

I love my dad so very much,
He cooks my dinner and my lunch,
He is always working up in Glasgow,
But when he comes back I love him so.

Grace Rutter (11)
Temple Moor High School, Leeds

Family And Friends

Family and friends mean the world,
Even when their hair is curled,
Brothers and sisters are the best,
Even when they've been a pest.
Mums and dads they treat us well
Even though we give them hell.
Nanas and grandads really care,
Even when I bake and don't share.
Friends are always there
We paint our nails and do our hair.

Sophie Eddleston (13)
Temple Moor High School, Leeds

Friends

What matters to me?
I'm thinking.
Friends, it has to be.
We laugh, we cry we're always together.
Secrets are shared and promises are made.
We laugh at random things
For example, this poem.
We are funny, freaky friendly girls
A few words might help.
And then it comes to the weekend.
Where we organise days out
Cinema, walks or even going to McDonald's.
The reason friends are so special is.
They're there for the rest of your life.
We're almost together 24/7.
We're like a cake with icing.
Never apart.

Jessica Holmes (11)
Temple Moor High School, Leeds

Love

Love, love, love is in the air
You may not see it,
But you can certainly feel it.

Mum, Dad you mean so much to me!
Brothers, sisters can't you see what you mean to me.

Grandma, Grandad love you lots,
Even though you make me wash the pots!
Just because I love you!

Jade Brogden (11)
Temple Moor High School, Leeds

All About Me

One of the things that matters to me,
is purely my family!

I really like to eat food,
especially if I'm in the mood!

I enjoy being asleep,
Best if I'm in it deep!

I like having fun,
that excludes eating buns!

Best of all is my pants,
they keep me warm and safe from ants!

My favourite place is Wales,
It's better than the Yorkshire Dales!

But then there's me,
Who's about as funny as Jack Dee!

Amy Rhodes (11)
Temple Moor High School, Leeds

My Mum

She raised me from birth,
That matters to me,
I love her so much,
I hope she can see,
That all she's done,
Has helped me grow,
Like flowers and sun,
Thanks Mum!

Keira Louise Makin (11)
Temple Moor High School, Leeds

Shoes!

Shoes can be pink,
Or purple or blue,
Shoes can be silver,
Or gold for you!
Shoes can be flat,
Or shoes can have heels,
Some shoes have diamonds,
But some shoes have wheels!
My shoes are black,
With sparkly bows,
Her shoes are red,
And show her toes!
So next time you go,
To buy some shoes,
Think about it . . .
Which ones should you chose?

Annabel Tree (11)
Temple Moor High School, Leeds

Family Poem

I love my family they are special and great,
They are funny in a kind of loving way.
Although you want to scream and shout,
No matter what we say they're always there for us at the end of the day.
What can we say, they are our family and they love us in every way.
Brothers and sisters no matter what you have,
They're always going to drive you mad.
Still they are loveable to have.
Some families are embarrassing to have, either way we love them a lot.
Embarrassing dads and caring mums,
Where would we be without them?
Family is special; they will never make you feel unsettled.
We love them lots.

**Lucy Vaughan, Shannon Charnley, Ellen Foulds,
Melissa Francis & Nikki Patel (13)**
Temple Moor High School, Leeds

Family And Friends

Family and friends matter to me because . . .
They love me, cuddle me,
Snuggle me.
Blow bubbles to me.
They are great to me!
Family and friends matter to me because . . .
They care for me,
Share with me.
They are great to me,
And they love me.
Family and friends matter to me because . . .
I love them,
Care for them,
Share with them,
They are the best!

Christina Gierke (11)
Temple Moor High School, Leeds

Future

Life,
Bright, dark.
That's the choice?
A choice you make, choose safely,
Love, peace.
Not danger, hate, war.
If, always if.
If you choose safely, love, peace.
There will be no forestation,
No depression,
No dark faces.
If you choose, danger, hate, war.
There will be no forests,
No happiness,
No bright faces.
This world is a piece of metal,
That is bound to rust.

Olivia Davey (12)
Tollbar Edge Cleethorpes Academy, Cleethorpes

Friends

Golden
Stars, midnight sky,
Shining brightly
Always there for you -
Even when you can't see . . .
They are there but,
If you take them for granted
They will disappear.
They'll be gone,
Evaporate into the dark night sky
Forever,
Never coming back.

Jess McGinlay (12)
Tollbar Edge Cleethorpes Academy, Cleethorpes

That's Unlucky

If you grow up with violence,
They expect you to be violent,
To people you care about,
It's all you ever hear about,
That's unlucky!

If you grow up in a place with murders,
They expect you to have at least attempted to murder someone,
What? Someone you care about,
You think about it all the time,
It's always in the back of your mind.
That's unlucky!

If you grow up with drugs,
What? They expect you to do drugs,
Hurt people you care about just to get your kick,
Most of you don't really know just how dangerous it is,
You could die or just be high
For what other reason than to just look fly
You're unlucky!

If you grow up in a ghetto,
They expect you to be ghetto,
Dress like a tramp,
And carry weapons,
Being a hoe to try and make tuppence,
To feed your children,
That's a good mum,
When all the dad is
Is a lousy bum.
You're unlucky!

If they grew up with all of this,
And what? They got out of all of this,
They left people they care about,
That's something you never heard about,
Now they have a better life,
A proper job and earn true money,
So they're still alive and are
Very lucky!

Mellissa Morrow (15)
Tollbar Edge Cleethorpes Academy, Cleethorpes

Abandoned

Lying, alone
The street, cold,
Warm-hearted, hoping someone
Will find me.
Curling,
In a,
Ball waiting for
Food to appear.
A
Child walking
Towards me, reaching
Her hands out to
Pick me up, backing off
Until I realised she loved me.
She slowly reached out for me.
New,
Home, new,
Family, warmth, a
Bed to lie on,
Food to eat, toys to
Play with all day all night,
I love my new home.

Shannon Gamble (12)
Tollbar Edge Cleethorpes Academy, Cleethorpes

Jack

Fluffy,
Warm-hearted,
Ball of fun,
Remembering the day we got you!

Jack,
That's you,
Born on Grandad's birthday,
April 5th, what a special day,
Grandad's gone but I've got you.

Jack.
We love you,
Just like Grandad too.
We love you both,
Thanks for the best dog
He's named after you.
Jack I love you and I always will!

Alicia Clarke (12)
Tollbar Edge Cleethorpes Academy, Cleethorpes

What Matters . . . World War II

W ar was taking over,
H itler's hatred hit them all.
A rmy troops risk their lives,
T he sound of the bombs was a deafening scream.

M en marched mightily to the battlefields,
A rmy soldiers stood in line ready to attack.
T heir lives at risk,
T hey had no choice, it was for their country.
E verybody was affected.
R ememberance day, to remember those who fought for us.
S ilence, on 11th November to show respect for the bravery of others.

Lillie Carrie (12)
Tollbar Edge Cleethorpes Academy, Cleethorpes

It Doesn't Feel Real

I had a dream, it didn't feel real
It had shrunk, it didn't feel real
But now, it hasn't grown, but not shrunk
You were there for him, now you've gone
It doesn't feel real
You've had treatment for ages now, radiotherapy
You seem fine, but we all know it's just an act
But, it still doesn't feel real.

You're my favourite, my godfather
You son might not know who you are
But you're standing strong, doesn't feel real
Even if we talk about it, I cry
It scares me, it still doesn't feel real
You should have gone to the doctor's when it started
This is why it doesn't feel real
It's all there in front of me, but I can't bring myself to believe.

Katie Willerton (14)
Tollbar Edge Cleethorpes Academy, Cleethorpes

Abuse

She hugged her knees
She begged, 'Stop . . . please'
He swung his fist
Barely missed.

She cried in pain
She felt so slain
He swaggered away
He's had his play.

His love had gone
It once had shone
The tears she cried
Escaping from her eyes . . .

Holly Andrews (16)
Tollbar Edge Cleethorpes Academy, Cleethorpes

191

Nothing Matters

Nothing matters to me
What matters to you
Can you tell me what matters to you
Because nothing matters to me.

If there's something matters to you can you
Tell me too because nothing matters to me.

Can you tell me. What matters to you in your life
Or in the school and in the world.

There is nothing in my life, in the world
And in the school that matters to me at all.

So what matters to you as nothing matters to me in life,
School and in the world at all.

If there is not something that matters to you then
That is alright but thanks for your help.

Martin Harper (14)
Tollbar Edge Cleethorpes Academy, Cleethorpes

I Love Him

Lovely
Cheesy grin
I love him
Toys piled up high
My little brother
I wouldn't have no other
Curly blond hair
Hazel eyes look up and stare
Pretending to be a car
Lazy not walking far
My little brother
Cheesy grin
I love him!

Millie Gallagher (13)
Tollbar Edge Cleethorpes Academy, Cleethorpes

The War

The war hurts many people like mums and dads, wife, kids,
Best mates and so on.

War kills us all no matter who you are. Even people that want
To stay out of the war and death are involved.

It kills us not by death but by losses and fear that we might
Die as bombers swarm over head with bombs that are like a hurricane.

Men on the frontline sacrifice their lives to defend our scared
And sacred country as the Nazi scum tear us apart with their
Dreaded bombs we quickly run for cover in our Anderson shelters.

We wear our gas masks after the dreaded bombs had
Exploded so we wouldn't die from the deadly smoke and gas.

I can't wait for the end of the war, I get to be reunited with
My mum if I can find her in the mounds of rubble and wreckage.

Ryan Booth (11)
Tollbar Edge Cleethorpes Academy, Cleethorpes

Family Matters

F amily are the best thing
A mazing is just one of the words to describe them
M any people are in families
I n many ways I love them
L ots of happy memories
Y ou'd be surprised how helpful they are.

M y family is the best
A lot of good things from the past
T remendous abilities each one has
T houghtful and beautiful
E veryone should love their families
R espectful in every way
S uper, spectacular and spontaneous.

Megan Brown
Tollbar Edge Cleethorpes Academy, Cleethorpes

What Matters

W ar covers countries as people fought for countries.
H orrible Hitler's hatred filled the air.
A iming guns at another army to win.
T he planes swarmed over head like a million seagulls.

M en marching looking brave but really petrified.
A stonished people watching wounded people.
T he sound of bombs like thunder but ten times louder.
T his is war.
E vacuated children switching countries.
R apid rifles rattled like a hamster biting metal cage bars.
S cared people hiding in shelter.

Abbie-Rose Raworth (12)
Tollbar Edge Cleethorpes Academy, Cleethorpes

What Matters

W orld War II matters
H earing air raid sirens, people ran to their
A nderson shelters
T o hide from the bombs

M any children were evacuated to
A countryside
T o escape the bombs and
T he war
E very soldier played a part to stop the
R aging war to
S ave people.

Jack Smith (11)
Tollbar Edge Cleethorpes Academy, Cleethorpes

Goal!

Bang!
A kick in the ribs
Flying through the air
The crowd like ants, blurred
Exploding
A white net, waiting still
Crashing like a rocket.
The net catches me
A thousand voices cheer
Goal!

Jordan Taylor (12)
Tollbar Edge Cleethorpes Academy, Cleethorpes

What's Wrong With Being Me?

Criticised for being me
Being different, standing out from the crowd
Football I love, bullied for being me.
Playing football with boys when I'm a girl.

What's wrong with being different?
What's wrong with playing a sport that we love?
Why can't people be themselves without getting ridiculed?

Why am I different for kicking a ball?
What's wrong with being me?

Olivia Harvey-Massey (14)
Tollbar Edge Cleethorpes Academy, Cleethorpes

My Dog

Tyler,
My dog,
Playful and cute,
He makes me smile,
Gulps all his food down,
As small as a Labrador puppy,
Playful and fast,
My dog,
Tyler.

Katie Pye (12)
Tollbar Edge Cleethorpes Academy, Cleethorpes

Who Am I?

I am alone, yet with my friends
I am excited, yet afraid
I am confident, yet unsure
I am hidden, yet in the open
I act without thinking, yet without acting
I believe in what I do, yet do not like what I am doing
I am loyal to my country, yet not always to myself
I look after my equipment, yet it doesn't always look after me
Who am I?

Craig Clephane (14)
Tollbar Edge Cleethorpes Academy, Cleethorpes

Young Writers Information

We hope you have enjoyed reading this book - and that you will continue to enjoy it in the coming years.

If you like reading and writing poetry drop us a line, or give us a call, and we'll send you a free information pack.

Alternatively if you would like to order further copies of this book or any of our other titles, then please give us a call or log onto our website at www.youngwriters.co.uk

Young Writers Information
Remus House
Coltsfoot Drive
Peterborough
PE2 9BF
(01733) 890066